BODY & SELF

Partners in Movement

Sandra Cerny Minton, PhD
University of Northern Colorado

Human Kinetics Books
Champaign, Illinois

Library of Congress Cataloging-in-Publication Data

Minton, Sandra Cerny, 1943-
   Body and self : partners in movement / Sandra Cerny Minton.
    p.   cm.
   Bibliography: p.
   Includes index.
   ISBN 0-87322-219-9
   1. Movement education.   I. Title
   GV452.M56   1989   88-30383
   613.7'1--dc19   CIP

Developmental Editor: Marie Roy
Production Director: Ernie Noa
Copy Editor: Claire Mount
Proofreader: Karen Leszczynski
Assistant Editors: Holly Gilly and Robert King
Typesetter: Angela Snyder
Text Design: Keith Blomberg
Text Layout: Denise Peters
Cover Photo: Bill Scherer, Centennial Photo, Greeley, CO
Cover Design: Jack Davis
Interior Art: Lotus McElfish
Interior Photos: Bill Scherer, Centennial Photo, Greeley, CO
Models: Lance Mangham, Lori Nakata, Mary Ordonio, Dea Wheeler
Printed By: Versa Press

ISBN: 0-87322-219-9

Printed in the United States of America

10 9 8 7 6 5 4 3 2 1

Human Kinetics Books
A Division of Human Kinetics Publishers, Inc.
Box 5076, Champaign, IL 61825
1-800-DIAL-HKP
1-800-334-3665 (in Illinois)

To all of the teachers, students, friends, and colleagues who have given me support and encouragement through the years.

Contents

Preface

Young children are at home in their bodies, but many adults are not. Locomotor activities and creative movement play come naturally to the child, but adults must be retrained in these activities if they are to perform them with spontaneity and grace. By the time many people reach adulthood, their bodies have become foreign objects.

Experiences in teaching dance at the university level for almost 20 years have brought me to this realization. Learning dance movement patterns requires a subtle knowledge of the body and its potential for movement in various joint areas. It requires being at home with one's body. Perhaps a renewed knowledge of our bodies should precede learning more complex movements involved in dance or learning any detailed motor sequence or sports skill. In other words, the individual needs to befriend his or her body through the exploration of simple actions before embarking on a study of more difficult activities.

The information in this book has been shaped by my personal experiences; it is drawn from a variety of disciplines such as kinesiology, dance education, the body therapies, and psychology. The intent is to offer this information in a format that is easy to understand so that the reader can quickly begin to integrate the information into daily life. The book begins on a concrete level with a discussion of basic anatomy and gradually progresses to less concrete and more imaginative concepts. The connection, however, between all chapters is an increased awareness of self and body. Throughout, the reader is encouraged to look at the body from a new perspective, to explore these new perceptions through simple movement activities, and to connect the dynamics of the body with the mind and the imagination. Much of the information presented in this text is part of dance classroom experiences. This content is extracted from the context of dance and applied to activities of daily life.

The following information is directed toward those who are involved in movement/learning situations, whether the activity is dance or sport. Chapter 1 summarizes how the body is put together. The skeleton, joint connections, and muscular configurations are described to create a clear picture of basic anatomy. Differences in body type as they relate to movement are also explained. Knowledge of structure leads into a discussion of movement potential, or the kinds of actions possible in joint areas throughout the body.

Chapter 2 deals with basic principles of effective posture and movement. These principles are used in the dance classroom, but can be easily applied to other areas of movement education and sports skill training. Attention is given to the concepts of stretching and strengthening, particularly as they relate to the anatomical knowledge presented in chapter 1. The information in the first two chapters should give the reader a clear picture of the body's natural potential for movement so that exercise without injury is possible.

Each person develops habitual movement patterns as he or she goes through life. Chapter 3 is included to help the reader bring these patterns into focus and see them in a new light. Daily actions such as walking, lifting, and climbing are described followed by suggestions for performing these activities with increased mechanical efficiency. An explanation of the elements of movement—space, time, and energy—is provided in this chapter as a framework from which to evaluate movement. The elements are discussed and then applied to the evaluation of (a) the efficiency of action and (b) the effectiveness of nonverbal communication through posture and gesture. Examples are given of how space, time, and energy can be used to analyze both efficiency and effectiveness of an individual's movement. Chapter 3 ends with group experiences in exploration designed to emphasize the nonverbal aspects of human communication.

Chapter 4 involves the use of the imagination as a tool to improve movement ability. The kinesthetic sense is described and brief examples of kinesthetic ability testing follow. The subject of imagery is then introduced as the link between mind and body. Both visual and kinesthetic imagery are described, and experiences connecting the kinesthetic and the visual are provided. Many suggestions are made for the use of visual and kinesthetic imagery as methods to improve alignment and movement ability. Anatomical images, mental pictures, the kinesthetic image of energy flow, and body image are all discussed. This chapter concludes with some information on (a) using the right brain to enhance body awareness and movement accuracy and (b) exploring creative movement experiences that use various forms of imagery as the connection between mind and body.

Acknowledgments

I would like to express my appreciation to Lance Mangham, Lori Nakata, Mary Ordonio, and Dea Wheeler, who posed for the photographs in this book.

I would also like to thank Dr. Carolyn Cody, professor, and Dan Libera, head trainer, University of Northern Colorado; Dale Lee Niven-Cooper and Marge Phillips; and Sally Kondziolka and Tara Steppenberg, Naropa Institute, for the many suggestions and words of encouragement they provided after carefully reading this text.

I am also grateful for the careful attention given to the photographs by Bill Scherer, to the illustrations by Lotus McElfish, and to the typing of final copy by Vicki Mossman.

Chapter One

Knowing Your Body

We progress through our lives in bodies that many of us know little about. In childhood, our bodies are a connection to the world—a tool for exploring the environment. Watch a young child use his or her body and its movements to investigate the surroundings, and you will see the importance of movement in the world of the young. The mimetic response of the infant to its parent is another example of the importance of the body for the child. All communication occurs through gesture, posture, touch, and facial expression, creating a natural connection between infant and parent.

As we grow into adulthood, the body/environment connection disappears. Our bodies become functional objects—the tools for transporting us on a daily basis and for accomplishing needed tasks. Use of the body as an expressive tool for communicating becomes buried in the past. The verbal, literal, and cognitive worlds take over in the learning process.

Many forms of physical exercise are currently in vogue, with aerobics, running, and walking being the most popular forms of participation. People taking part in these activities often know little about body structures. Many individuals perform these exercises correctly, but just as many can be seen repeatedly doing incorrect patterns. There is a tendency among some to force the body into directions and to shape it into positions in which it is not supposed to go. Participants frequently ignore correct use of the body—a use that is in agreement with the natural potential for movement that does exist.

The information presented in this book evolved from careful thought and from many years' experience teaching dance at the college level. Through these experiences, I began to see that many adults were out of touch with their bodies. Many times a movement sequence, single action, or position demonstrated in class was not interpreted and performed properly by a majority of the students. Problems in use of space are, of course, easiest to spot and analyze. As students attempted to copy movements, the spatial aspects of direction, level, and size were changed from the model. A foot pointed directly to the front became for some students a diagonal point; an arm held to the side on a shallow forward diagonal was often placed on a diagonal behind the body. For many the body held forward from the hips in a parallel position to the floor was reproduced higher or lower than the desired parallel (Figure 1.1). Students often misrepresented and changed the use of time and energy as well, but these mistakes are more difficult to analyze and describe.

These classroom experiences led me to a number of conclusions, one of which was that people needed to be more aware of their bodies and of the natural potential for movement that exists within their innate structure. A basic understanding of the anatomical aspects of kinesiology would be a helpful prerequisite for students involved in movement participation classes. This prerequisite applies to dance, individual sports, and team sports, so that the learning of more complex movement patterns is introduced together with information on the body's basic potential for movement. Practicing and exploring simple actions is one way of creating a better understanding on a body level. Such explorations of the body's potential for movement could lead to an awareness of the physical aspects of self.

This chapter begins with a discussion of the physical structure of the body and normal potential for movement in various joint

a   b

Figure 1.1.   Body shape and placement: (a) correct position and (b) incorrect position of head and arms.

areas. Exercises are described for exploring the possibilities for action at the joints. Differences in body structure are pointed out, because these differences affect movement potential.

The Skeletal System

The skeletal system provides a framework for the body. The bones of the skeleton connect, or articulate, at places known as *joints* to form the entire network.

Bones

The human skeleton is made up of many separate bones. The size and shape of these bones suits their function and placement in the body. Bones bearing greater weight are larger and more dense, whereas those bearing less stress are smaller and lighter. An example of a bone that supports more weight is the thigh bone or *femur*. In comparison to the bone of the upper arm, the *humerus*, the femur is much heavier and larger in size, although both bones make up the upper segment of an extremity. Increased bone size and density are also found in the vertebrae,

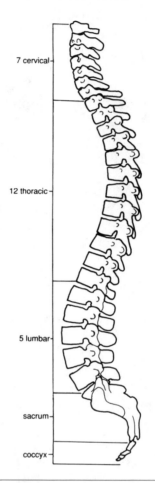

7 cervical

12 thoracic

5 lumbar

sacrum

coccyx

Figure 1.2.   Bones of the spine, side view.

or separate bones of the spine. As one moves down the spine, the vertebrae become larger to support increased body mass from above (Figure 1.2).

The function of a bone determines not only its size, but its shape as well. The *vertebrae* can be compared to rounded building blocks that are stacked to form the spinal column enclosing the spinal cord. In contrast, the ribs are slender and gracefully curved to form a protective cage around the organs of the chest; the thin bones of the skull grow together in childhood to enclose the brain's mass in a spherical chamber. Bones used to move the body are long and slender to accommodate actions of various lever systems (Figures 1.3, 1.4, and 1.5).

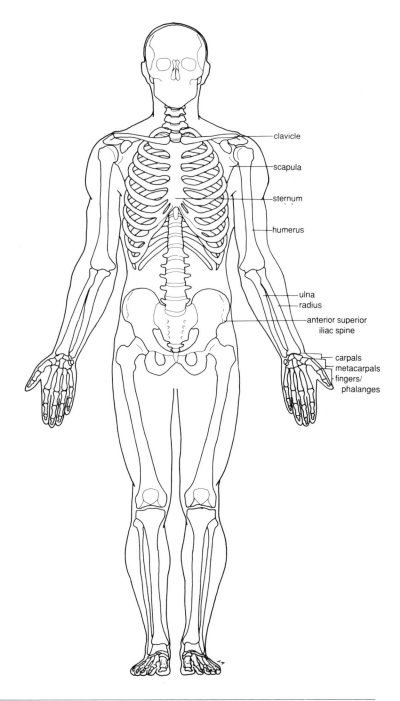

Figure 1.3.   Skeleton, front view.

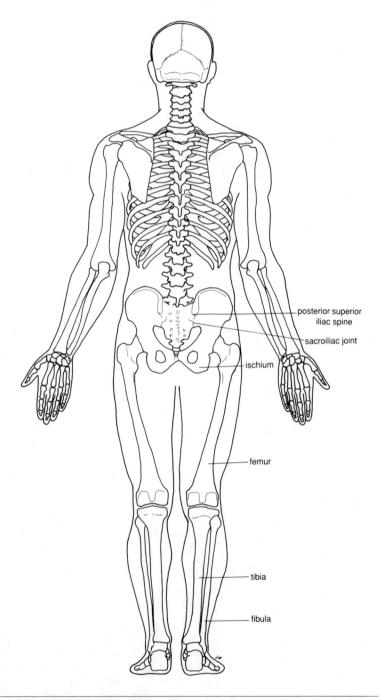

posterior superior
iliac spine

sacroiliac joint

ischium

femur

tibia

fibula

Figure 1.4.   Skeleton, back view.

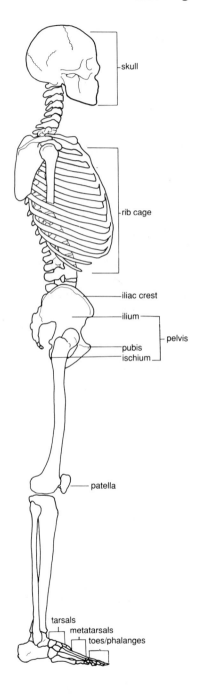

Figure 1.5. Skeleton, side view.

The organization of the human skeleton is a feat of natural engineering. Those bones that form the core of the body—the head, chest, and pelvis—are known as the axial skelton. The bones of the legs and arms are the appendicular part of the total framework.

Axial skeleton.   The skull sits atop the entire skeletal framework. It is made of separate bones that are held in almost direct contact with each other by a thin layer of connective tissue. Those joints that are immovable and with which the bones are in almost direct contact are known as *sutures* (the differences in joint structure will be discused in more detail later). The sutures of the skull are designed for structural strength, not movement. The *clavicle* is positioned at the front of the shoulders beneath the neck. It is a long narrow bone that extends horizontally from the body's midline outward to the tip of the shoulder. The *scapula* is a flat triangular bone located in the upper back; it can be easily felt or palpated. In some people the scapula protrudes outward from the body producing a winged effect. The clavicle and scapula together form a structure called the *shoulder girdle* (Barham, 1978; Figures 1.3, 1.4, and 1.5).

A flat and somewhat dagger-shaped bone is found on the front of the body along the midline. This bone is called the *sternum*. The *ribs* articulate at the front with the sternum and wrap around to the back to connect with the vertebrae of the spine to form a cagelike structure enclosing the organs in the thoracic area. There are 12 pairs of ribs in the body (Figures 1.3, 1.4, and 1.5).

The spinal column runs the full length of the upper and lower portions of the body. The separate vertebrae are positioned one on top of the other to produce its entire length. There are 7 separate vertebrae in the neck or cervical area, 12 in the thoracic or chest and rib cage area, and 5 in the lumbar region or lower back. The *sacrum* and *coccyx* lie below the lumbar spine and are formed from bones that are fused together. In each portion of the spine the vertebrae are arranged in a curve rather than being positioned in a straight line. When viewed in profile, the cervical curve reaches forward, the thoracic curve extends backward, the lumbar curve repeats the forward curved shape found in the cervical area, and there is another backward curve in the region of the sacrum and coccyx (Figure 1.2). The spinal curves help to alleviate some of the stress of weight bearing that would otherwise extend straight through the back. Compensatory curves have been developed in the spine to attain movement, because a straight back would not be suited to carry off-center or lateral loads like the head or thorax. A flexible support column has developed to carry laterally distributed weights, because it curves in a direction opposite to that which the load is actually bending the spine (Todd, 1975). Thus the thoracic curve reaches to the back so as to counterbalance the lateral weight of the thorax at the front of the body.

The lower portion of the spine connects with and forms part of the pelvis. Two separate hip bones form the sides and front of the pelvis, with the sacrum and coccyx completing the pelvic structure at the back of the hip area (Barham, 1978). The underside of the pelvis is formed from a third bone, the *ischium*. In adulthood the separate pelvic bones have ossified and grown together to form a shallow cuplike structure encasing the organs located in the lower part of the body (Figures 1.3, 1.4, and 1.5).

Appendicular skeleton.   The bones of the arm consist of the *humerus* in the upper arm and the *radius* and *ulna* located in the lower arm or forearm. The wrist is composed of eight small bones known as *carpal bones*, whereas the *metacarpals* form the body of the hand, and the *phalanges* make up the fingers (Figures 1.3 and 1.10).

The thigh bone or *femur* is the longest and largest bone in the body (Barham, 1978). The bones of the lower leg segment, the *tibia* and smaller *fibula*, are located beneath the femur, and the *patella* or knee cap is found at the front of the knee joint (Figures 1.3, 1.4, and 1.5). The lower ends of the tibia and fibula plus some of the seven separate bones known as the *tarsals* make up different parts of the ankle. The tarsals also form the arch of the foot, whereas the five *metatarsals* are found in the ball of the foot. The five toes or digits are made up of the *phalanges* (Figure 1.6).

A good way to learn the placement and shape of the separate bones is to make a tracing of the skeleton. One tracing is made

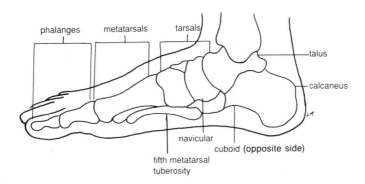

Figure 1.6.   Bones of the foot.

of the front view of the skeleton, and another of the back view. These tracings can be done from the illustrations that appear in Figures 1.3 and 1.4. As you trace the separate bones, concentrate on their shape and placement and on how they connect or articulate with other bones.

Joints

The bones of the human skeleton are connected at many points known as *joints*. Some of these joints allow movement and some do not. Joints may be classified by structure and by the kinds of movement allowed. Structure will be discussed first, followed by an explanation of movement planes. Finally, the joints are classified in terms of movement potential.

Classification by structure. A *fibrous joint* is one in which the bones are connected by a thin layer of connective tissue, so that the bones are almost directly in contact with one another (Hinson, 1977). The bones of the skull are immovable, because they are sutured together by fibrous joints.

A second type of joint is formed from bones and intervening discs of fibrocartilage (Hinson, 1977). *Cartilaginous joints* permit only a light amount of movement, but provide great strength. They can be found between the pubic bones and between the vertebrae of the spine.

The type of joint that provides for the most movement potential has a more complex structure than the fibrous or cartilaginous joints already mentioned. It is known as a *synovial joint* (Hinson, 1977). Synovial joints have a space between the ends of the bones, which is filled with *synovial fluid*. The ends of the bones are usually flared outward and covered with *cartilage*, and the entire joint is surrounded by a *fibrous capsule* or membrane (Hinson, 1977; Figure 1.7). *Ligaments* or bands of connective tissue extend between the bones providing stability. They hold your bones together and, though pliable, are not as elastic as muscle fibers. Some people have very loose ligaments and other people's are much more tightly strung together (Alter, 1983). The *tendons* of various muscles also cross joints and attach to bone; they increase the strength of the capsulelike structure (Figure 1.8).

Movement. Kinesiologists classify human movement into two basic categories: *linear* and *angular*. If actions follow a straight line, they are linear (Barham, 1978). A human being is performing linear movement when he or she skates straight across ice.

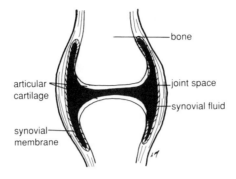

Figure 1.7.   A synovial joint and capsule.

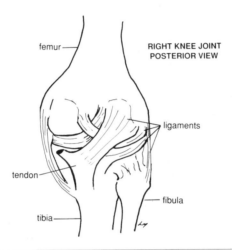

Figure 1.8.   A joint and the surrounding ligaments and tendons.

Movement tracing a curved pathway in space is angular (Barham, 1978). A cartwheel is an example of angular motion because the performer's hands and feet go through an arc in space. Joint movement potential can be either linear or angular in nature. The difference between the two forms of activity is that linear movement occurs in a line in a plane, whereas angular movement takes place in a plane around a central point or axis (Hinson, 1977).

The human body is intersected by three planes. Division of the body front from back is by the *frontal plane*. The *sagittal plane* divides the right side of the body from the left, and the *horizontal plane* divides the top of the body from the bottom (Figure 1.9). Movement occurs in these three planes, or in planes parallel to these three.

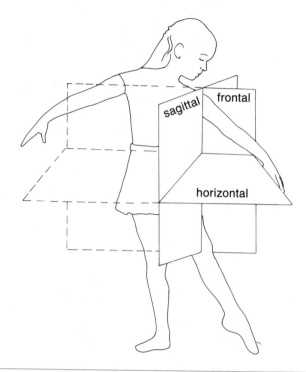

Figure 1.9. Three planes of motion: frontal, sagittal, and horizontal.

Classification by movement.   Kinesiologists, or those who study the structure, function, and movements of the human body, classify the various joints by the kind of movement or movements each type allows. The possibilities for movement constitute the joint's potential for motion. The following discussions are derived mainly from Hinson's (1977) *Kinesiology.*

Joints that allow for linear movement only are called *nonaxial.* In nonaxial joints the articulating bones simply glide or slide over one another rather than moving around a central point or axis. Such gliding can, however, take place in all three planes. An example of a nonaxial joint would be the articulation between some of the bones in the foot. The connection between the talus, calcaneus, and navicular allows a linear or sliding action (Figure 1.6). Likewise, most of the carpal bones that form the palm of the hand glide or slide against each other (Figure 1.10).

An *uniaxial* joint permits angular movement in a single plane around a fixed point or axis. Uniaxial joints are sometimes known as *modified hinge* or *double condyloid* joints. The elbow and the knee are examples of a uniaxial joint (Figure 1.11).

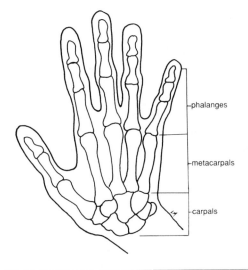

Figure 1.10.   Bones of the hand and wrist.

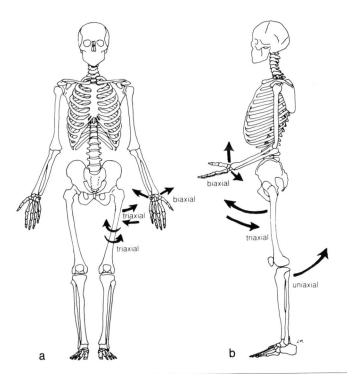

Figure 1.11.   Planes of movement possible at the wrist, hip, and knee: (a) one plane for the wrist and two planes for the hip; (b) other plane of movement for wrist and hip, as well as the single plane of movement at the knee.

Biaxial joints are those that provide for motion in two planes around two perpendicular axes. The wrist is a biaxial joint (Figure 1.11).

Triaxial joints permit movement in all three planes (sagittal, frontal, and horizontal) and around three axes. Due to their shape, triaxial joints are sometimes called ball-and-socket joints. The hip and the shoulder joints both have a triaxial structure. In each of these, the ball-shaped end of one bone fits into a cup-shaped socket on the articulating surface (Figure 1.11).

The point here is that knowing the structure of the different joints provides for more enlightened movement participation. Movement can be learned and then performed within the framework of the body's potential for action. Forcing or twisting joints into directions for which they are not structured should be avoided to prevent injury.

The Muscular System

The muscular system lies over and is connected by tendons to the skeletal framework. Figures 1.12 and 1.13 show the superficial muscles on the front and back of the body. As you study the muscles, note their size, shape, and placement. Find the beginning and ending of each in the drawings. The human body has many muscles, but only the larger and/or more superficial of these will be discussed here. The discussion begins with those muscles located in the shoulder area.

Shoulder

The *pectoralis major* is a large flat muscle on the front of the chest and shoulder. Its fibers are arranged in the shape of a fan and extend from the clavicle, sternum, and ribs to a point on the front and outside of the humerus. A much smaller and deeper muscle, the *pectoralis minor*, is located beneath the major. It extends from the front of the third, fourth, and fifth ribs to a protruding portion of the scapula (Figures 1.14 and 1.15). The cap-shaped muscle at the top of the shoulder is called the *deltoid* and reaches from the outer third of the clavicle, the tip of the shoulder, and the spine on the scapula to a midpoint on the outside of the humerus (Figure 1.13).

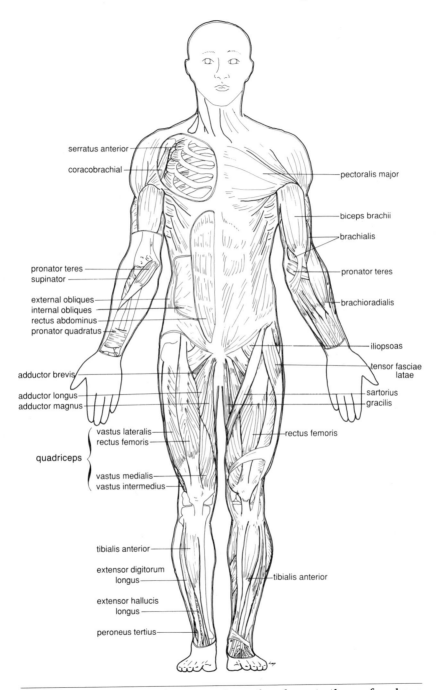

Figure 1.12. Muscles, front view (muscles closer to the surface have been left out on one side of the drawing to expose the deeper muscles beneath them).

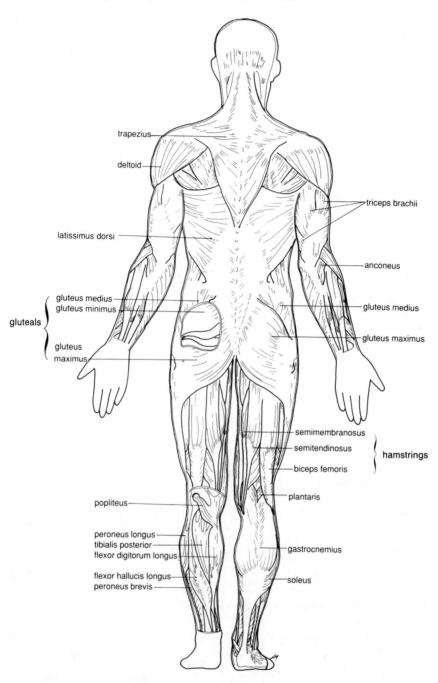

Figure 1.13. Muscles, back view.

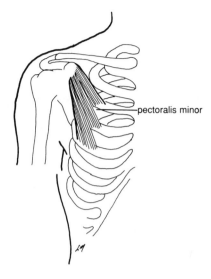

Figure 1.14.   Pectoralis minor (covered by pectoralis major).

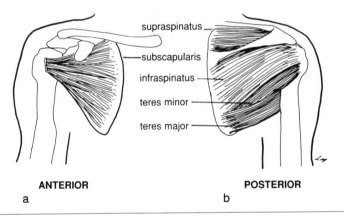

supraspinatus

subscapularis

infraspinatus

teres minor

teres major

ANTERIOR

POSTERIOR

a

b

Figure 1.15.   Muscles of the scapula: (a) front and (b) back.

The *trapezius* is one of the larger and more superficial muscles of the neck and back. It is flat and triangular in shape and extends from the base of the skull and the spine in the neck, shoulders, and upper back to the tip of the shoulder and outer portion of the scapula (Figure 1.13). Another muscle of the shoulder area is the *serratus anterior*, which wraps around from the side of the upper nine ribs to the underneath surface of the scapula. The serratus is attached to the ribs in a sawtooth fashion (Figure 1.12).

Front of the Body

The abdominals are a group of large flat muscles located on the front of the body. The most external or superficial of these is the *rectus abdominis*. Its fibers run along the middle of the body in a vertical direction extending from the sternum to the lower and middle part of the pelvis. The two sides of the rectus are separated by a broad tendinous band. The oblique abdominals can be found beneath the rectus. There are two sets of obliques, both of which run in diagonal, but opposite, directions. The *external obliques* extend from the ribs on one side of the body to the top of the pelvis on the same side. The *internal obliques* are found beneath the externals and connect the top of the pelvis to the lower four ribs, again on the same side of the body. Diagonal placement of the obliques makes it possible for them to assist in rotating or twisting movements in the torso (Figure 1.12).

The psoas, iliacus, and quadratus lumborum are deeper muscles of the lower body. The *psoas* is made up of two parts—the major and the minor. It is deep in the abdomen running from the lowest thoracic and all the lumbar vertebrae to the femur, where it crosses the front of the hip joint. The *iliacus* also extends in front of the hip from the pelvis to the femur. Frequently, the psoas and iliacus are said to be a single muscle called the *iliopsoas* (Hinson, 1977). The *quadratus lumborum* spans the space between the bottom of the last rib and the top of the pelvis (Figure 1.16). It is a major stabilizer of the lumbar area of the spine.

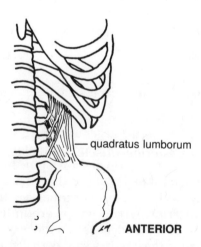

— quadratus lumborum

ANTERIOR

Figure 1.16. Quadratus lumborum (located on either side of the spine beneath a fatty area of the body).

Back of the Body

A superficial muscle found in the lower back is the *latissimus dorsi*. It is a very broad muscle wrapping around from the lower thoracic, lumbar, and sacral spine and lower three ribs to a point on the front of the humerus (Figure 1.13).

Many smaller muscles connect points on the spine to nearby structures in the body or to other locations on the spine itself. The *prevertebral muscles* run from the front of the cervical and first three thoracic vertebrae to the lower portion of the back of the skull, the *scaleni* extend between the upper two ribs and the sides of the cervical vertebrae, and the *sternocleidomastoids* are found on both sides of the neck between the sternum/clavicle area and the lower jaw (Figure 1.17).

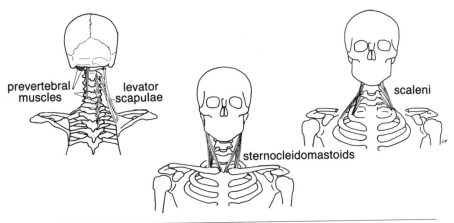

Figure 1.17.   Deep muscle groups of the neck region.

The *splenius, suboccipitals, erector spinae,* and *semispinalis* are other muscle groups found in the neck and back. Each of these groups is made up of separate muscles that are long and thin in shape and that extend from points on various vertebrae to points higher up on the spine or to the base of the skull (Figure 1.18). The *deeper posterior muscles* of the spine connect points on one vertebra to a point on another vertebra near it. They are thin short muscles (Figure 1.19).

Arm

The large muscles of the upper arm and forearm are also important in most types of activities. The *biceps brachii* is located

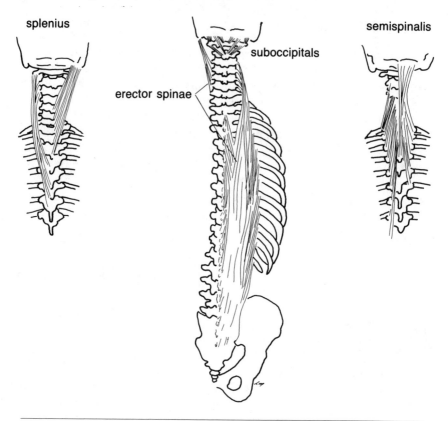

splenius

semispinalis

suboccipitals

erector spinae

Figure 1.18.   More muscles of neck and back.

on the front of the upper arm. It has two parts, both of which extend from two different points on the scapula to the radius. Opposite the biceps on the upper arm is the *triceps brachii*. The triceps has three parts, all of which are on the back of the upper arm. The longest of these three parts crosses the shoulder joint running from the outside of the scapula to a point on the ulna in the lower arm. The other two parts of the triceps cross only the elbow joint (Figures 1.12 and 1.13). The flexor and extensor muscles of the forearm are shown in Figure 1.20.

Other smaller muscles of the arm consist of the *brachioradialis*, *brachialis*, *pronator teres*, *pronator quadratus*, *supinator*, and *anconeus*. Each of these muscles provides a different connecting link in the arm. The brachioradialis, brachialis, pronator teres, anconeus, and supinator all run between points on the humerus across the elbow to various points on the radius or ulna. The pronator quadratus spans the radius to the ulna at the lower end of both of these bones (Figures 1.12 and 1.13).

Figure 1.19. Deep posterior muscles of spine.

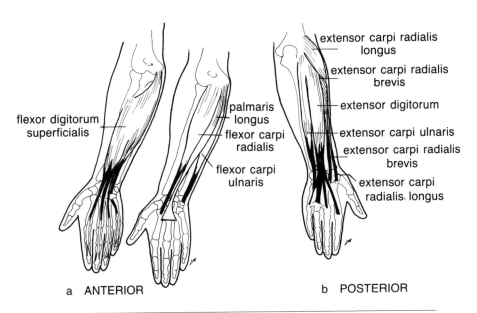

a ANTERIOR   b POSTERIOR

Figure 1.20. Muscles of forearm: (a) front and (b) back.

Leg

The *quadriceps* muscle group forms the curve at the front of the thigh. It is made up of four separate muscles—the *rectus femoris* and the three *vasti muscles* (Figure 1.12). The rectus is the most superficial of the quadriceps group extending from the lower portion of the pelvis across the front of the hip to the knee cap or patella. The three vasti cover the front and sides of the thigh from points high on the femur to the patella.

Several more narrow muscles lie on the front and side of the thigh. One of these, the *sartorius*, runs diagonally from the outside of the pelvis to a point on the upper and inside part of the tibia or large bone of the lower leg. The two others, the *tensor fasciae latae* on the outside, and the *gracilis* on the inside, extend from points low on the pelvis to the lower leg below the knee (Figure 1.12).

The *adductor muscles* are located on the front and side of the thigh. The three adductors—the magnus, longus, and brevis— all originate from points on the lower part of the middle of the pelvis and extend to different places on the inner surface of the femur (Figure 1.12). The *pectineus* is a very deep muscle that crosses the inner side of the hip joint. It is found in the groin area beneath the rectus femoris and the sartorius and crosses from the lower pelvis to the inner portion of the upper femur (Figure 1.21).

The muscles of the buttocks are the *gluteals*. The *gluteus maximus* is the largest and most superficial of the three. It originates along the back of the pelvis, as well as along the sacrum and coc-

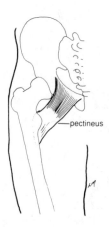

Figure 1.21.   Pectineus (beneath rectus femoris and sartorius).

cyx, and inserts on the back and upper part of the femur. The *gluteus medius* lies under the maximus and the tensor fasciae, whereas the *gluteus minimus* is under the medius. The medius extends from the back of the pelvis to the outside of the top of the femur. The minimus goes from the back of the pelvis to the front of the top of the femur (Figure 1.13).

The three *hamstrings* make up the muscle group at the back of the thigh. The *semitendinosus* begins at the middle and lower part of the back of the pelvis and extends to the inner and front surface of the tibia. The *semimembranosus* originates at a similar point on the pelvis and ends at the inside and back of the tibia. The *biceps femoris* also extends from the lower middle part of the back of the pelvis, but goes to the outside of the tibia and fibula instead (Figure 1.13).

The *outward rotators* are another muscle group located at the back of the hip. This group includes six very deep muscles that cross from the front and back of the pelvis and sacrum to the upper part of the femur (Figure 1.22). They include the *piriformis, obturator internus, obturator externus, quadratus femoris, gemellus superior,* and *gemellus inferior.*

Many additional muscles are located on the front and the back of the lower leg. Some of these are more superficial than others. The *gastrocnemius* is found in the calf at the back of the lower leg. It extends from the back lower portion of the femur and runs the full length of the calf to the Achilles tendon at the back of the ankle. The *soleus,* located beneath the gastrocnemius, begins at the upper part of the tibia and fibula. Like the gastrocnemius, it inserts into the Achilles tendon, but does not cross the back of the knee joint (Figure 1.13).

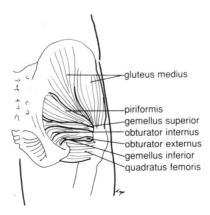

Figure 1.22.   Outward rotators, back view.

Some smaller muscles are situated at the knee. These include the *popliteus* and *plantaris*. The popliteus is a small, very deep muscle at the back of the knee. It runs from the back and very lower part of the femur to the back upper portion of the tibia. The plantaris is a long, narrow muscle between the gastrocnemius and the soleus, extending from the back and lower femur to the back of the calcaneus or heel bone (Figure 1.13).

A group of small muscles surround the ankle joint on the front, back, and sides of the leg. The *tibialis anterior* runs from the outside and upper tibia down the front of the lower leg to the inner and under side of the arch of the foot. The *extensor digitorum longus* again begins on the lower leg bones, the tibia and fibula, but extends in a straighter downward direction to the phalanges of the second, third, fourth, and fifth toes. Beginning lower on the front of the fibula, the *extensor hallucis longus* runs all the way to the base of the last bone of the big toe. The *peroneus tertius* is difficult to distinguish from the extensor digitorum longus. It originates on the lower third of the front of the fibula and ends on the upper surface of the base of the fifth metatarsal in the foot. Two other peroneal muscles are the *peroneus longus* and the *peroneus brevis*. The longus, the more superficial of the two, begins on the head and upper part of the fibula and runs to the outer and underneath surface of the foot, whereas the brevis extends from the lower two-thirds of the fibula to the outside of the base of the fifth metatarsal (Figures 1.12 and 1.13).

Three additional small muscles surround the ankle at the back of the lower leg: *flexor digitorum longus*, *flexor hallucis longus*, and *tibialis posterior*. The flexor digitorum longus goes from the back of the tibia to the ends of the four smaller toes, the flexor hallucis longus from the lower two-thirds of the back of the fibula to the end of the big toe, and the tibialis posterior from the back of the tibia and fibula to various points on bones in the arch and metatarsal area (Figure 1.13).

Many small muscles are located in the foot. Called *intrinsic muscles*, they are arranged in layers to provide connections between the bones in the arch, metatarsals, and phalanges.

A good way to remember the configurations of muscles is to take your tracing of the skeleton (front and back) and draw in the muscles over the bones. Use a different colored pen to sketch in the muscles. Note the size, shape, and placement of muscles as you draw. Be aware of how each muscle is positioned in relation to a joint and the direction in which fibers are arranged. You should now have a clear picture of the location of both the bones and the muscles of the body. This picture is important to understanding the possible movements or movement potential

of various joints. The *Anatomy Coloring Book* by Kapit and Elson (1977) is an excellent reference to help you understand the
structure and placement of bones and muscles in the body.

Muscles and Movement

By now you should realize that the muscles and their tendons
span the joints of the body. Each muscle has its own characteris-
tic shape. Some are long and narrow; others are rather short.
Regardless of shape, all muscles are made up of varying numbers of fibers and are connected to bones at either end by way
of tendons. Additional stability is given to a joint by the ligaments
that surround it and hold it in place.

Contraction.   Movement is produced at a joint when muscle fibers
contract or shorten (Figure 1.23). This type of muscular action
is called *concentric contraction*. Muscles also produce movement
through lengthening while gradually giving into gravity or
another force, and such action is known as *eccentric contraction*.
The potential for movement existing in a particular joint is determined by several factors: (a) joint structure and its potential
for movement, (b) location of a muscle or muscle group with
respect to a joint, and (c) the direction the fibers run within a
muscle. Knowledge of joint structure must be combined with an
understanding of muscular arrangement around that joint in
order to envision movement potential in a particular body area.
The following examples should clarify these ideas.

Muscular action at joints.   The elbow is a hinge or uniaxial joint.
This means that the elbow can move with angular motion around
one axis and in one plane; its structure permits no other possibilities. It is also important to go back to the analysis of muscula-
ture surrounding the elbow to understand movement potential

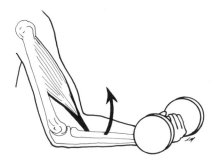

Figure 1.23.   Muscle and tendon attachment spanning elbow.

here. Remember that the biceps brachii runs down the length of the upper arm at the front of both the shoulder and the elbow (Figure 1.12). If you picture a shortening of the fibers of this muscle (concentric contraction) when the elbow is straight at the side of the body, it is easy to understand how this shortening can cause the elbow to bend. A lengthening of the biceps brachii (eccentric contraction) would allow for the opposite movement, or a straightening of the elbow to occur, because it would allow the lower arm segment to give in gradually to gravity. Other muscles that cross the front of the elbow aid in the bending action.

A similar analysis is possible with muscular action at the hip. The hip is a triaxial joint and has three possible planes of action. The rectus femoris of the quadriceps group is connected by its tendinous attachments across the front of the hip and knee (Figure 1.12). In a standing position, shortening contraction of the rectus femoris and other hip flexors would cause the hip to bend, so that the thigh would reach into the sagittal plane in front of the body. Likewise, a lengthening contraction would allow for a return to a position with the hip straight. The rectus femoris and the three vasti cross in front of the knee. A concentric contraction of these muscles would move the knee joint from a bent to a straight position.

The adductor muscles and their tendinous attachments cross the hip joint and are located in the region of the inner thigh. If you were lying on your back with your feet in the air and your legs together above your torso, an eccentric contraction of the adductors would allow the legs to separate gradually, opening to a position forming the shape of the letter V above your body. This movement takes place in the horizontal plane. A return from this position requires a concentric contraction of the adductors against the pull of gravity in order to pull the legs back together again.

A good way to understand muscular action is to reread the preceding section that describes muscle shape, position, and location. As you read about a muscle find it on the appropriate illustration, noticing where it begins and ends; whether it is in front, behind, or at the side of a joint; and in what direction the fibers run, such as vertical, horizontal, or diagonal, in relation to the nearest joint. The three preceding factors together with movement potential in a joint are your clue to understanding muscular action. A few more examples may help your understanding here.

The deltoid is a cap-shaped muscle that crosses the top of the shoulder. The fibers in the middle portion of this muscle run straight across the top of the shoulder to a point on the side of the upper arm. The concentric contraction of these fibers aids in lifting the arm to the side of the body.

The hamstrings and its tendinous attachments span the back of the hip and knee. Again, a concentric contraction, or shortening of these muscles, would initiate a straightening action at the hip, while causing a bending at the knee.

Farther down on the back of the leg, the gastrocnemius and soleus provide similar examples. A review of the placement of these two muscles reveals that the more superficial of these two muscles, the gastrocnemius, has tendinous attachments crossing both the knee and the ankle. The soleus connects to the same tendon at the ankle, the Achilles, as does the gastrocnemius. Concentric contraction of the gastrocnemius causes the knee to bend. Both muscles, however, operate to initiate a straightening of the ankle (i. e., pointing the foot).

A final example should suffice. You will remember that the different sets of abdominal muscles are located at the front of the torso. Three of these sets run in vertical and diagonal directions. A concentric contraction of the vertical abdominals, or rectus abdominis, causes the torso to bend or curve forward into the sagittal plane. The two sets of diagonal or oblique abdominal muscles, in contrast, assist in torso twisting actions, because of the diagonal rather than vertical positioning of their fibers.

Paired muscle groups. Paired muscle groups can be found throughout the body. This is another trait of the body's structural organization. It means that a muscle located on one side of a joint is matched or paired with another muscle situated on the opposite side of that same body part. Examples are easily found throughout the human muscular network (Figures 1.12 and 1.13).

Examples of Some of the Muscle Pairs

1. Biceps brachii
   (front of upper arm)
   Triceps brachii
   (back of upper arm)

2. Rectus abdominis
   (front of body)
   Long muscles of the back

3. Quadriceps
   (front of thigh)
   Hamstrings
   (back of thigh)

4. Tibialis anterior
   (front of lower leg)
   Gastrocnemius, soleus
   (back of lower leg)

5. Thigh adductors
   (inside of thigh)
   Gluteus medius plus other muscles
   (outside of hip)

Because the location of a muscle is related to its joint action, it would stand to reason that muscles on opposite sides of a limb perform opposite kinds of movements, and this is true. The biceps and triceps are found on opposite sides of the upper arm. Biceps contraction causes the elbow to bend. A lengthening contraction of this same muscle allows for straightening, because it uses the force of gravity to accomplish this action. A more forceful straightening of the elbow (more forceful than one initiated by the pull of gravity) must be accomplished through a shortening contraction of the triceps (Hinson, 1977). This opposition of muscle action exists throughout the body. A muscle and its opposite pair are sometimes called *antagonists* (Luttgens & Wells, 1982). If one muscle contracts, it is necessary for the antagonist to relax and lengthen to permit the action caused by the muscular contraction to happen.

A muscle has tendinous attachments extending to two different bones. The muscle originates on the more stable of the two bones and extends outward from the body's center to a point on the less stable bone. The less stable of the two bones usually moves when a muscle contracts. The rectus femoris, for example, crosses in front of the knee joint, and its contraction straightens the knee by moving the lower leg (Figure 1.12). Stabilizing the lower leg by planting the foot on the floor would cause the rectus to move the thigh to straighten the knee (Hinson, 1977). To analyze movement, you must know which bony segment is free to do the moving.

One other point concerning muscular action is important to the functioning of two joint muscles. Because this type of muscle crosses two joints, it has the capacity to initiate action in either joint. The rectus femoris crosses the front of both hip and knee. Contraction of the rectus could cause movement of either of these joints, although its capacity to move the hip is more secondary to the contractile ability of other muscles that move this joint (Hinson, 1977). There are other two-joint muscles in the body, such as the biceps brachii, triceps brachii, and gastrocnemius (Figures 1.12 and 1.13). Check your understanding of the functioning of these muscles at each of the two joints that they cross.

Identification of Movements

Kinesiologists have specific names for the action or actions of each of the joints in the body. As you learn these actions relate them to (a) joint structure, (b) axes and planes of movement, and (c) location and direction of muscle fibers.

Narrowing the angle between two bony segments is called *flexion*. When you begin from anatomical position, flexion occurs in the sagittal plane or in planes parallel to the sagittal. It is possible to flex at the shoulder, elbow, hip, knee, and spine (Figures 1.24,

Figure 1.24. Shoulder flexion.

Figure 1.25. Elbow flexion.

Figure 1.26.   Knee flexion.

Figure 1.27.   Forward flexion of spine.

1.25, 1.26, and 1.27). Narrowing the angle at the front of the ankle so that the foot moves in the sagittal plane is known as *dorsiflexion* (Figure 1.28). Bending the spine to the side in the frontal plane is called *lateral flexion* (Figure 1.29).

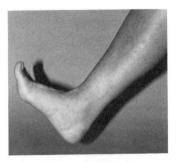

Figure 1.28. Ankle dorsiflexion.

Figure 1.29. Lateral flexion of spine.

Extension is a return from flexion to a straight joint position. Extension occurs in the sagittal plane and involves widening the joint angle (Figure 1.30). Extension of the ankle is plantar flexion at that joint (Figure 1.31). To go beyond normal extension is to hyperextend. *Hyperextension* is sometimes required in an activity, but should be done with care for the sake of joint safety. In some people hyperextension of the spine, knees, and even elbows is possible, although it puts added stress on the joint or joints. When necessary, hyperextension should be done in the cervical and thoracic parts of the spine, and not in the lumbar

Figure 1.30. Extended position of shoulder, elbow, hip, knee, and back.

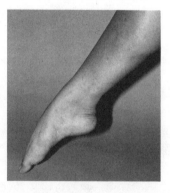

Figure 1.31. Ankle plantar flexion.

portion of this structure. In hyperextension joints take on a bowed appearance (Figures 1.32, 1.33, 1.34, and 1.35).

Movement away from the body's midline into the frontal plane is called *abduction*, whereas a return in this same plane toward the midline is *adduction*. Abduction can take place at the shoulder, hip, ankle, and wrist (Figures 1.36, 1.37, and 1.38). (Technically, the movements of the wrist away from and toward the body's midline are known in kinesiological terms as *radial* and

Figure 1.32. Hyperextension of shoulder.

Figure 1.33. Hyperextension of hip.

ulnar deviation.) The hand in a palm-down position is *pronation*. The palm-up position is *supination* (Figure 1.39). These actions do not take place in the wrist, but are the result of a rolling action of the two bones in the lower arm segment (Barham, 1978). Lifting the outer border of the foot is *eversion*; lifting the inner

Figure 1.34. Hyperextension of both knees.

Figure 1.35. Hyperextension of lumbar spine.

border is *inversion* (Figure 1.40). To roll inward on the arch of the foot without lifting the outer border is to pronate. Outward rolling, or supination, causes the foot to look curved, in contrast to inversion, in which only the inner border of the foot is lifted (Figure 1.41).

Figure 1.36.   Abduction at shoulder.

Figure 1.37.   Abduction at hip and shoulders.

Rotation is the same as twisting in a joint. This action occurs in the horizontal plane and can go in outward and inward directions. It is possible to rotate both the shoulder and the hip (Figures 1.42 and 1.43). Rotation can also take place in the spine as several or more vertebrae twist around the long axis running vertically through this structure (Figure 1.44).

Some additional examples should clarify the relationship between joint structure, muscular configuration, and movement

Figure 1.38.   Abduction at wrist and ankle (kinesiologists call these actions *radial* or *ulnar deviation* in the wrist).

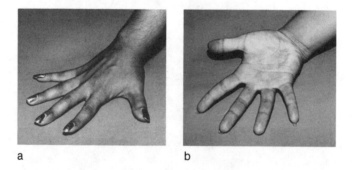

a   b

Figure 1.39.   Movement of hand and wrist: (a) pronation and (b) supination.

potential. The knee is a modified hinge or uniaxial joint allowing for motion in one plane, the sagittal plane. The movement potential of the knee is flexion and extension. Muscles performing these two actions must cross the knee either in front of or behind the joint and must have fibers running in a vertical direction. A concentric contraction of muscle fibers at the back of the knee causes flexion; an eccentric or lengthening contraction of this same muscle or muscles initiates extension or release into

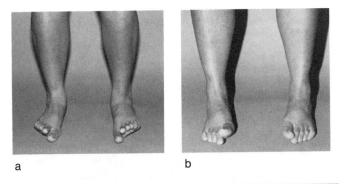

Figure 1.40.   Lifting the borders of the feet causes (a) eversion and (b) inversion.

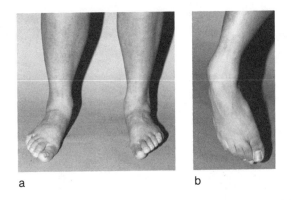

Figure 1.41.   The foot can be (a) pronated and (b) supinated.

gravity. A more forceful extension would have to be activated by concentric contraction of the muscles at the front of the knee.

The hip has a much greater potential for movement than the knee. Movements of flexion, extension, hyperextension, abduction, adduction, and inward and outward rotation are all possible here. As has already been explained, muscles that perform hip flexion must span this joint in a vertical direction and in front of it. Their concentric contraction causes the thigh to be lifted into flexion in the sagittal plane. A return from flexion to extension could easily be accomplished through an eccentric contraction of these same muscles. A more powerful extension of the hip is produced by concentric contraction of other muscles behind the joint. This latter group run vertically across the back of the hip. Movement from side to side—abduction and adduction—brings the muscles at the inside and outside of the hip into play.

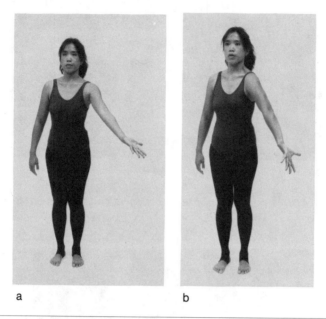

a   b

Figure 1.42.   Rotation (a) outward and (b) inward.

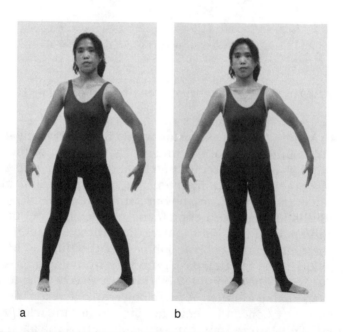

a   b

Figure 1.43.   Rotation (a) inward and (b) outward on right side.

Figure 1.44. Rotation of spine.

Concentric contraction of the muscles crossing the hip at the inner thigh produces adduction; concentrically contracting those
muscles that run vertically at the outside of the thigh initiates
abduction. Inward rotation is initiated by concentric contraction
of muscles spanning the inside of the hip with fibers running in
a horizontal or diagonal direction. Outward rotation, by contrast,
must be activated by muscles at the back of the hip where a concentric contraction of their fibers produces this action. Both inward and outward rotation occur in the horizontal plane.

Structural Differences

Differences in structure affect the way you move; they provide
you with variations in movement potential. The most basic
understanding of structural variation is drawn from the three
types of physique: *endomorph, mesomorph* and *ectomorph* (S.
Fitt, personal communication, summer, 1982 [class notes]). The
endomorph's body has more fatty tissue and is soft and rounded
in appearance. Endomorphs must work to acquire endurance and
control their weight. Mesomorphs have heavy muscles, are short-
er with dense bones, and have to stretch a lot to increase movement range. The ectomorph is more loosely put together and
must work hard to develop strength and endurance (Figure 1.45).

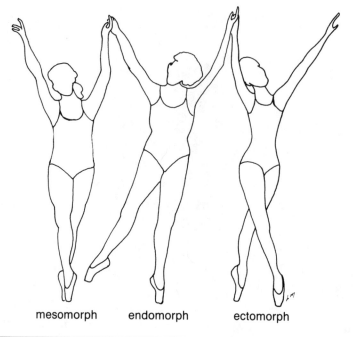

mesomorph   endomorph   ectomorph

Figure 1.45.   Three body types: (a) mesomorph, (b) endomorph, and (c) ectomorph.

In terms of movement, the mesomorph is more adept at darting movements, quick turns, and jumps. Ectomorphs enjoy movement performed at a much slower pace, because it feels comfortable on their less compact bodies.

Many other structural differences affect how you move. Males, for example, have narrower hips and a more direct energy connection between pelvis and femur than females. Females have a larger angle in the articulation at the hip joint (Figure 1.46). Males, thus, can run faster, but have less range of movement in outward rotation at the hips.

A wide variation also exists in torso length among individuals (the torso is the body area from sternum to waist). Some people have a long torso and short legs; others are endowed with a short torso and long limbs. Lateral flexion and forward curving or flexion of the spine are easy for those with a long torso. They are more difficult actions for the person with a short torso, because he or she does not have as much space in which to perform this motion. The mover with the short torso and long legs, on the other hand, can reach his or her limbs out into various directions with great range in use of space and can easily increase the length of each step to move forward more rapidly.

Figure 1.46. Hip width differs between male and female.

The curves of the spine also differ from person to person. These differences can be seen in the side view of an individual. A large lumbar curve causes the upper body to be carried to the back with the weight on the heels. In rapid movement forward there is a tendency for the lumbar curve to increase even more, causing the upper body to go even farther behind the hips. Other variations in the spine include large cervical or thoracic curves, a forward head, and a very flat sacrum. Each of these deviations limits the use of one's full movement potential.

Finally, some people have very loosely jointed bodies. This usually means that their bones are not strung together very tightly—a deviation that allows for a larger range of motion in joint areas (S. Fitt, personal communication, summer, 1982 [class notes]).

Explorations of the Body's Potential for Movement

It is fun and relaxing to explore movement potential at the different joint areas in the body. The following movement sequences are provided for such activities. Some of these exercises can be performed in a sitting position, whereas for others you need to lie on the floor, or if necessary on a comfortable mat. As you move through these explorations, try to visualize the skeletal and muscular structures with which you are working. Do each exercise slowly so that you fully experience the action and feel continuity throughout the motion. You might like to play some soft soothing music as you proceed through each exploration. It is important to relax and focus on your body before you begin. Close your eyes when possible during explorations, because this enhances concentration on self and cuts out distracting visual stimuli.

In the first sequence, you could sit on a chair or on the floor with your legs crossed. Close your eyes and concentrate on one shoulder. Visualize the structure of this shoulder. Lift the shoulder up as close to your ear as you can. Slowly return your shoulder to its original position. Lift your shoulder toward your ear again and let it drop quickly back to normal position. Explore other directions by taking the same shoulder back behind your body, down below normal level, and in front of your body. Each time bring your shoulder back to its center position. Next, connect the four directions already explored by moving your shoulder continuously through the upward, backward, downward, and forward directions. You will trace a circle with your shoulder at the side of your body. Reverse the direction of your circling once you have done it backwards several times. Finally, try the shoulder circles with your arm lifted in abduction. Be aware of the different feeling of space and weight as you circle with your arm in abducted position. Rotate your shoulder while your arm is still lifted to the side. See whether you can rotate farther in a forward or backward direction. Try shoulder rotation with your arm reaching in other directions, and be sure to work both shoulders.

Move your mental focus to your head and neck for the second sequence. Keep your eyes closed and take your head slowly forward, to the side, backward, and to the other side. Feel the heaviness in your head as you perform this exploration. Next, connect the four directions described by executing slow and continuous circling through them. Notice points of tension or tightness as you circle. Make sure to circle your head in both directions, and then return to center. With your head remaining level, twist your neck around its axis, so that your face turns from side to side. Be aware of the amount of twist you have in your neck, and see if you can twist farther on one side in comparison to the other.

Next, bring your concentration to your back while you remain seated with your eyes closed. Again explore all four directions, allowing your upper back to flex forward, lateral flex to the side, and extend or hyperextend backwards. (To be safe, limit hyperextension to the upper back.) Connect these directions again by performing a circle. Try the exercise in both directions and then come back to center. Twist slowly from right to left, checking the degree of twist on each side.

a   b

Figure 1.47.   Exploration: (a) assume starting position and (b) slowly flex spine, returning to (a).

The fourth exploration is done while you are sitting in a chair with your feet slightly apart and flat on the floor, hands on thighs, and eyes closed. Move to your lower or lumbar spine, and let it round with your body slumping forward. Return to a vertical or centered position. Do this bending and straightening action slowly several times. Breathe in as you sit up and out as you round forward. Do not go beyond normal extension of your back into hyperextension (Figure 1.47).

You can also practice curving the lower part of your spine in a different manner. Close your eyes again, and round your back so that you are sitting way back on your hips. Return to a position with a straight back, and repeat the curving and lengthening several times (Figure 1.48). How does this form of spinal curving differ in body feeling from the curving described in the preceding paragraph? Judith Aston has developed a system of repatterning the body. She calls this form of spinal curving arcing and uses it as an action to be practiced as part of her body correctives system (J. Aston, personal communication, summer, 1983 [class notes]).

As you sit, try shifting your weight from one hip to the other. Do this slowly at first and then faster. Let your hip shifting get larger so that the movement travels up your spine. You should feel sequential waves of motion from side to side as the shifting causes changes higher in the body (Figure 1.49).

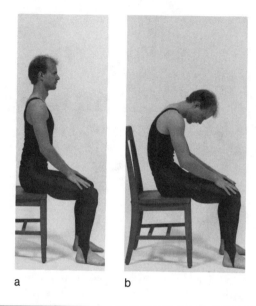

a   b

Figure 1.48.   Exploration: (a) sit forward on chair to begin and (b) slowly flex spine and return to (a).

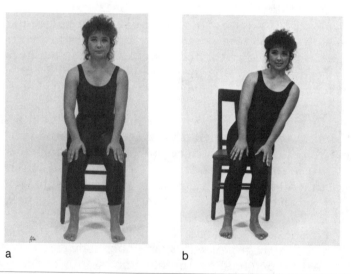

a   b

Figure 1.49.   Exploration: (a) sit with weight on both hips and (b) slowly shift weight from one hip to the other.

Lie down on your back, placing both feet slightly apart flat on the floor with the knees bent (Figure 1.50). Close your eyes and keep your knees bent. Start to slide one leg away from your hips, and as you do so pick it up an inch or two off the floor. Then

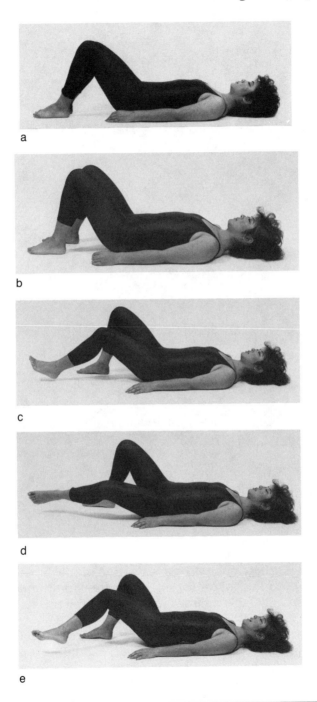

Figure 1.50. Exploration: (a) begin in this position, (b) start to move one leg away from hip, (c) continue action in (b), and (d) then turn leg outward and (e) inward at hip.

c

Figure 1.51. Exploration: (a) assume starting position and (b) slide one leg away from hip, (c) so that hip and knee extend.

gently jiggle it from side to side. Your muscles should feel loose and free, and there should be a sensation of movement flowing in waves through your entire leg. Be aware of rotation in the hip joint as you jiggle the leg from side to side. Try the action in the other leg (Figure 1.50).

Return your legs to the position demonstrated in Figure 1.50a. Take one foot and slide it along the floor, extending the knee and hip. Let gravity help to pull your leg to the floor. When the leg is extended, pull it back flexing at the joints and returning to the original position. Remain as relaxed as possible throughout the action. Concentrate on the differences in muscular feeling while flexing and extending (Figure 1.51).

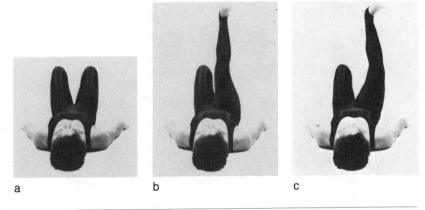

a   b   c

Figure 1.52. Exploration: (a) using same starting position as in Figures 1.50 and 1.51 (b) extend leg above hip, and (c) rotate hip outward and inward.

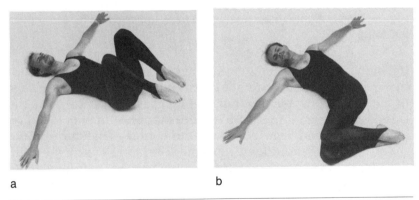

a   b

Figure 1.53. Exploration: (a) assume this position and (b) roll from side to side, allowing legs to fall to side.

Start from the same flexed joint position, bring one foot directly above your hip, and dorsiflex the ankle. The sole of the foot should be flat in relation to the ceiling, as if you were preparing to walk on it. Keep the ankle flexed and rotate the hip inward and outward. Be aware of differences in degree of rotation in each direction. Do these explorations on the other leg, and then fold both legs in toward the body (Figure 1.52). Gently roll from side to side on the hips. Allow the legs to fall naturally from one side to the other while leaving the arms on the floor at shoulder height. Notice how the side to side action triggers rotation in the lower part of the spine (Figure 1.53). End with both legs folded in toward

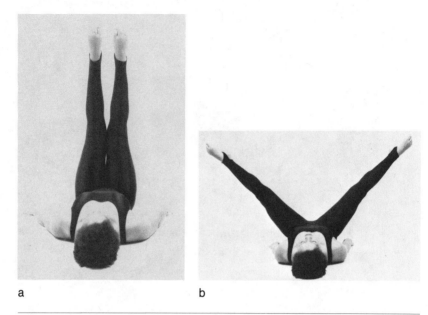

a   b

Figure 1.54.   Exploration: (a) starting here, (b) open legs to side, returning to (a).

the body. Finally, extend both legs directly above the hips with
the ankles and knees straight or extended. Slowly open the legs
to the sides from this position, feeling gravity pull down on the
legs as they open (Figure 1.54). Return to the starting position,
and then fold both legs in toward your center as in Figure 1.53a.

You can devise additional movement explorations for yourself.
Simply review the potential for movement in various joints, and
then perform patterns that go through the range of possibilities
found in each area. The ankle, for example, is another area that
could be explored.

Chapter Two

Being Aware
of Your Body

Total body awareness is based on understanding body structure and function. Principles such as alignment, centering, gravity, balance, breathing, and tension/relaxation can improve knowledge of how to move more effectively. A discussion and exploration of these principles is found in this chapter.

Alignment

The *alignment*, or posture, of the human body is important because it is the balance point from which all action begins. The well-aligned body is an efficient organic entity, and the individual with poor posture lives in a body that functions with stress and strain. Poor alignment at one point in the body reverberates throughout the whole carefully balanced structure, causing other body parts to shift to accommodate the problem. Muscles normally at rest in a body with good posture must work to pull bones into place to maintain a semblance of a well-balanced skeletal network. The bones are the weight-bearing parts of the body; they are constantly subjected to the force of gravity. Balance of the bones at their contacting surfaces at joints, together with muscular movement, must be understood to attain economical postural adjustment (Todd, 1975). By gaining balance at weight-bearing and weight-transferring points in the skeleton, we can equalize the pull on antagonistic muscles during passive conditions and therefore release more energy for use in action (Todd, 1975).

Assessment of Alignment

Problems in alignment are easy to spot. Some of the first things to look at are the individual body segments: head, shoulder girdle, torso area, and pelvis. In a well-aligned body each of these segments is balanced effortlessly on top of the other, and the pull of gravity is felt straight down to the floor. Todd (1975) described good alignment in a similar manner. She said that the ideal way of carrying oneself is to balance the body by piling up segments with the gravity axis passing through the center of the three main weight masses, the head, thorax, and pelvis. In this way muscles put out less energy, and the bones do their full share of work. You need only view the body from the side to judge the placement of each segment.

Analysis of posture is also done in a more detailed manner. Simply have the subject stand facing you with weight on both feet. The legs are turned slightly outward with arms hanging relaxed at the sides of the body. This is known as anatomical position (Figure 2.1).

You can begin your postural analysis by starting at either the top or the bottom of the body. Check the inner border of each foot at the arch. Some people carry their weight on the inside of the arch in a pronated position. Others have an outwardly rotated stance that can be discovered in a front view of the body, because both feet will be directed away from the midline of the body. Next move up to the lower leg segment. The larger bone of the lower leg is the tibia. In some it has a bowed appearance curving out-

Figure 2.1. Anatomical position.

ward away from the center of the body (S. Fitt, personal communication, summer, 1982 [class notes]). The knees may face straight ahead or may be turned slightly inward. In some individuals, body stresses have caused inward rotation of one knee while the other one faces directly forward. It is also important to see if the knees are at the same level.

Hip level should be checked as well. Sometimes you need to place the forefinger of each hand on the iliac crest on each side of the body to find out whether the pelvis rides level (Figure 2.2). An uneven pelvis has several causes such as differences in leg length or a curvature of the spine.

Uneven hips are usually accompanied by uneven shoulders, which can also be assessed in anatomical position. Finally, see if the head is carried in a vertical position, or if it is placed to one side or the other. Some specialists who do corrective work with alignment believe incorrect head placement can neurologically trigger other postural problems farther down the spine. The *Alexander Technique* of realigning the body, for example, is centered around correct placement of the head in relation to the rest of the body. In this technique, patterns of tension and poor coordination are related to imbalances of the head and neck (Gelb, 1981). This technique is also based on the premise of the body as both a physical and a psychological concept.

Figure 2.2. A test for level hips (place thumbs at same point on each side of pelvis).

Figure 2.3. Pronation, often accompanied by fat pads at outside of heel.

Turn to the back of the body and you will see some of the same problems in alignment from another angle. Rolling inward or pronation is accompanied by fat pads protruding at the outside of the foot (Figure 2.3). In some individuals weight is carried at the outside so that the foot and ankle are convex at the outside and concave at the inside (Figure 2.4). Check to see if weight placement is the same or different for each foot.

The level of the hips and shoulders and the angle of the head and neck can be checked from the back as well. It may be necessary to judge whether the hips are level by locating the sacroiliac

Figure 2.4.   Weight carried on one side of the foot often causes a hollow around the ankle.

Figure 2.5.   A test for level hips, from back.

joints, which appear as two dimples on the back of the pelvis. These joints are positioned at the articulation of the sacral spine and the pelvis. Place the thumb of each hand on one of these dimples to see if they ride at the same level (Figure 2.5).

It is imperative that you check posture from the side or profile view in addition to checking it from the front and back, because the profile reveals different structural and weight-bearing problems. Sometimes it helps in this evaluation to hold a string with a weight on it at the ear. This device, called a *plumb line*, is used by kinesiologists to judge posture because it coincides with the line of gravity as it passes down through the body to the floor.

Figure 2.6.   Measuring good alignment with plumb line.

Gravity causes the plumb line to be pulled directly to the floor. In good alignment, the line of gravity passes just behind the ear, through the center of the shoulder and hip joints, and a little in front of the ankle through the foot (Hawkins, 1964; Figure 2.6). Look at an individual in profile to see how close the ear, shoulder, hip, knee, and ankle come to an imaginary plumb line.

Start at the bottom of the body to see how weight is carried on the feet in profile. If the weight is carried forward, the lower leg segment leans forward, decreasing the angle at the front of the ankle; weight pushed back to the heels causes a widened angle. The knees may be in front or in back of the vertical line of the plumb line, indicating flexion or a backward bowing into hyperextension. Likewise, the hips are either in front or in back of the line of gravity. Someone with forward hips walks with a hip lead and the upper body tilted backwards. A hip-backward position encourages a walk with the upper body leaning forward and hips trailing behind (Figure 2.7).

A profile of the body affords an excellent view of the spinal curves and pelvic inclination. The placement of the hips in relation to the line of the whole body was discussed in the preceding paragraph, but the pelvis itself can be positioned at different degrees of inclination, particularly in a forward direction. When the anterior superior iliac spine is lower than the posterior superior iliac spine the individual has increased pelvic inclination; decreased pelvic inclination occurs when the anterior superior

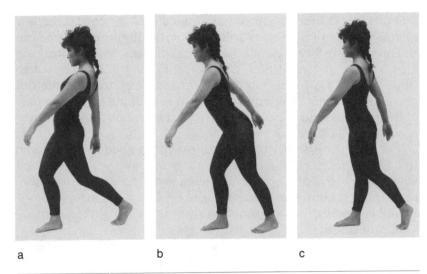

a   b   c

Figure 2.7. Walking with hips (a) thrown forward, (b) backward, and (c) in correct position (shoulders above hips).

iliac spine is higher (S. Fitt, personal communication, summer, 1982 [class notes]; Figures 1.3 and 1.4). Exaggerated pelvic inclination can be decreased through balancing exercises and visualization techniques. The degree of curvature in the lumbar, thoracic, and cervical areas can be evaluated, as they relate to the line of gravity. Some people have a rather large lumbar curve—a condition known as *lordosis*. A large backward curve in the thoracic spine is known as *kyphosis* and is usually seen in conjunction with a forward head and shoulders. If caught early enough, lordosis and kyphosis can be diminished through exercises that will bring muscles into balance. Check the degree of forward curve in the cervical spine, the placement of the shoulders, and the positioning of the head in relation to the line of gravity.

Alignment and Movement

Good alignment is dynamic, not static. It is not a rigid placement of the body frozen in space and time, but a position of readiness for movement.

Watch carefully while someone begins to walk or run, and you will notice that the entire body alignment tilts in a forward direction. In order to initiate forward motion, it is necessary to bring the weight to the front of the feet and allow the whole body to tilt forward into the line of direction. Try balancing your weight on both feet. Then slowly start to take a step forward on either foot. Be aware of how your weight and the alignment of the entire body shifts forward into the sagittal plane. Continue walking forward to experience how your weight shifts from one foot to the other and how your alignment must change in the direction of your movement. A common problem in walking is to leave part of the body behind or to lead with a part of the body once movement begins (Figure 2.7).

It is important when walking to maintain good alignment so that the segments of the body—head, trunk, and pelvis—remain stacked on top of one another. When a segment shifts out of line, movement becomes less efficient. Energy is wasted in an attempt to pull segments into alignment, rather than being used to motivate movement.

Practice walking slowly, and this time concentrate on the total alignment of your body. Have a feeling for your posture from the top of your head to your feet. Be aware of whether the segments of your body stray from good alignment. Try moving in other directions, such as to the side, backwards, and diagonally, and continue to be aligned. Gradually take your movement into a run, but keep your body in line. Good alignment becomes more difficult as momentum increases, because you are shifting farther from the center vertical position. In a run or leap, greater adjustment in alignment must be made, and this requires greater strength and control (Hawkins, 1964). It is important to develop kinesthetic or body awareness of posture while you are standing and moving.

Better alignment and posture can be achieved by balancing the body. This means stretching and strengthening appropriate muscles or muscle groups (S. Fitt, personal communication, summer, 1982 [class notes]). First, one needs to understand how to *stretch* a muscle in order to increase flexibility and how to *strengthen* it, because there are some basic differences between these two activities. Many people do not understand these differences and seem to confuse the two kinds of action.

Flexibility.   Stretching is a means to improve flexibility. It is a lengthening action, and as such it should occur along the direction of the fibers in a muscle or muscle group. It should feel good, not painful, and be experienced in the belly of a muscle, not at the ends of a muscle where tendons attach muscle to bone. Even people with loose ligaments need to feel a stretch sensation in their muscles; if they do not, stretching is not being done properly or body parts are not positioned correctly (Alter, 1983). Increased flexibility provides for greater range of motion in a joint area because joint potential is no longer restricted by muscular tightness. A more flexible body also provides some insurance against injury. Such a body is more giving and can go with the flow in many different kinds of movements and positions. During a fall, added flexibility allows the body to give and cushions against injury. Learn what proper stretching techniques feel like in your muscles.

Stretching can be accomplished in a number of ways. The most widely used method today is to ease the body into an appropriate position that produces a lengthening in the muscle fibers you wish to stretch. This position is held for about a minute and then released (Alter, 1983). Such a procedure is sometimes called *passive* stretching. Bouncing or *ballistic* stretching should be avoided, because it causes muscle fibers to contract instead of release. The body should also be moved some and warmed up preceding holding or passive stretches.

Stretching is brought about by eccentric muscular contraction as well. You will remember that movement is caused by shortening or contraction of muscle fibers, known as a concentric contraction. Movement can also be the result of a gradual lengthening of muscles, or an eccentric contraction, as body parts give in to gravity. An eccentric contraction of muscle involves lengthening and thus a stretching of muscle at the same time, even though the muscle is still somewhat contracted.

Another method of stretching is called *reciprocal innervation* of antagonistic muscles. In this method of stretching, the muscle group opposite the group you wish to stretch is contracted against resistance. This contraction is held in the midrange of motion at that joint for 10 to 20 seconds. The contracting muscles are then released, and the individual moves into a position that stretches the desired muscles, again holding in stretch position, this time for 30 seconds to 1 minute (S. Fitt, personal communication, summer, 1982 [class notes]). You may need a partner to help you with this stretching technique (Figure 2.8).

Strength. Strengthening requires an opposite muscular action in comparison to stretching. To strengthen, you contract a muscle. Preferably, this contraction takes place with added resistance to make the muscle do more work. It is best to condition for strength through the full range of motion of a joint (S. Fitt, personal communication, summer, 1982 [class notes]). There are various ways to cause muscles to do more work. One is to lift weights, or to put weights on limbs before beginning an

a

b

Figure 2.8. Stretch using reciprocal innervation of antagonistic muscles: (a) contract quadriceps against resistance and (b) relax quadriceps and stretch hamstrings.

exercise session. A way of building specific muscle endurance is to increase repetitions of a specific action. Finally, as is frequently done in dance classes, strength can be improved by holding a body part such as a leg off the floor against the pull of gravity (Figure 2.9).

Muscular balance. Balancing the body is accomplished by stretching and strengthening appropriate muscles or muscle groups. Muscles that have shortened need to be stretched; those that are elongated must be shortened through strengthening. Unfortunately, normal daily activity does not usually produce a muscularly balanced body; most people tend to be tight in some areas and weak or loose in others (Alter, 1983).

Figure 2.9. Strengthening by resisting gravity through holding.

Some examples should make this concept clear. Think again about the line of gravity as it runs along the side of the body. If an individual's shoulders fall in front of this line, the muscles at the front of the shoulders are contracted or shortened. Those at the back of the shoulder are lengthened and weak. To balance the muscles in this area and return to a better alignment, it is necessary to stretch muscles at the front and strengthen those in the upper back (Figure 2.10).

A similar instance is to maintain a flexed hip position when standing. Such a muscular configuration often develops in those who spend a lot of time sitting during working hours, and is due to a shortening of muscles crossing the front of the hip joint and a lengthening in those at the back. To reverse this placement of the body, the person needs to stretch (lengthen) at the front and strengthen (shorten) at the back. This balances the body and allows a return to a more vertical alignment (Figure 2.11). It is easy to see whether you are lengthening or shortening in a body area. Simply put two fingers on two points on the body and move to the desired or more aligned position. If the two fingers move farther apart you are lengthening, and if they come closer together you are shortening in that area of the body (Figure 2.12).

A word of warning is in order here. The goal of exercise should be to tone muscles, not to put excessive stress on ligaments, joints, and tendons (Alter, 1983). Ligaments and tendons should not be stretched because they will not return to their original length. Stretched ligaments and tendons produce overly mobile and unstable joints, which are injured more easily.

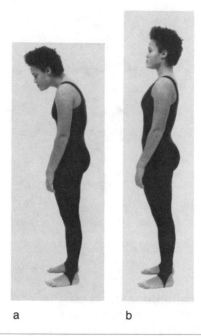

a   b

Figure 2.10.   Poor posture (a) caused by tight muscles at front of shoulder and (b) corrected by stretching muscles at front and strengthening those at back.

Evaluation of Flexibility and Strength

The following tests provide an opportunity to evaluate individual flexibility and strength, particularly as they relate to a balanced and aligned body. One must remember, however, that in testing for flexibility, tightness in an area could mean one of two things: (a) muscular tightness, or (b) structural limitations. Muscular tightness can be changed through stretching, but structural limitations are due to the way the body is put together and cannot be altered. Structural limitations refer to those produced by bones and ligaments. The bones of different people vary in size and shape, as do the joints between the bones. Some individuals have joints that allow a greater range of movement. The ligaments of some are also more loose than those of others. All testing should be conducted while the person being tested is wearing a minimum of clothing, such as a leotard, bathing suit, or shorts and T-shirt.

Tightness at the front of the shoulder has already been discussed. Such tightness is usually found among those with forward shoulders and a rounded upper back. Movement range or

a   b

Figure 2.11.   Alignment: (a) Bad alignment due to tight hip flexors; (b) improved alignment as a result of stretching hip flexors and strengthening hamstrings.

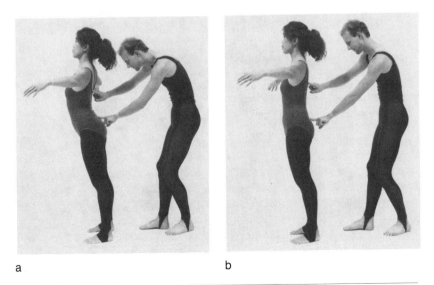

a   b

Figure 2.12.   Lumbar spine is (a) hyperextended; (b) correction of hyperextension produces greater length in back.

flexibility can be tested by lifting the arm in abduction to a position parallel to the floor. An inability to take the arm behind the body indicates tightness at the front of the shoulder in the area of the pectoralis major. If a person has trouble taking the abducted arm in front and across the midline of the body, tightness in the muscles at the back of the shoulder might be the cause.

Strength at the front and back of the shoulder can also be evaluated. Simply lift the arm again to the side and horizontally, and attempt to move it in front of the body while a partner resists your movement. Perform this same resistance test in the backward direction (Figure 2.13). The person helping you with this test should be able to tell you in which direction you were able to exert the most force. Ability to exert more force in a direction demonstrates greater strength in the contracting muscles. For example, to move the arm in front of the body you would have to contract the muscles at the front of the shoulder. If you were able to exert greater force to the front, then the muscles in front of the shoulder are stronger.

Tightness in the muscles of the back affects posture or alignment. Such areas of tightness can be seen from a side view of the body. Kneel down on the floor and lower and curl the body

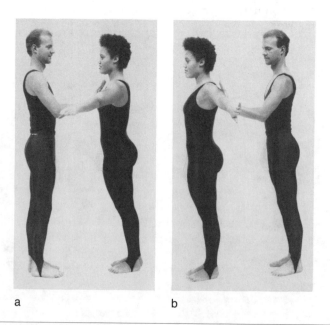

a   b

Figure 2.13.   Test for strength in muscles at front and back of shoulder: (a) resisting forward movement tests strength in muscles at front; (b) resisting backward movement tests muscles at back.

Figure 2.14. Flat areas may indicate muscular tightness.

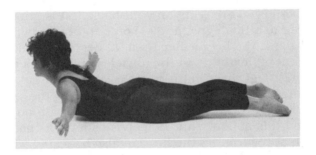

Figure 2.15. Test for range of motion at front of body.

forward (Figure 2.14). An observer at your side may see flat places in the spine indicating points of tightness (I. Dowd, personal communication, summer, 1981 [class notes]).

The area of the lumbar spine presents special problems for many. You can see tightness in this area by viewing the body from the side. A large lumbar curve could be structural, but could also indicate tightness when accompanied by a protruding abdomen. The position shown in Figure 2.14 will also show tightness in this back area. To test for range of movement at the front of the body, have the individual lie on his or her stomach and lift the upper body off the floor. Hips and legs remain on the floor (Figure 2.15). This same action tests back strength. An abdominal curl is a good test for strength at the front of the body (Figure 2.16). You may find that it is easier to lift to the back or to the front in each of these positions.

Testing for strength and flexibility in the muscles surrounding the hip is best accomplished while lying on the floor. (Note: The exercises described in this section were derived from S. Fitt, personal communication, summer, 1982 [class notes].) The muscles at the back of the hip, particularly the hamstrings, are tight in many people. To test for hamstring tightness, lift one leg up above

Figure 2.16.   Abdominal curl indicates strength at front of body.

the body while you are lying on your back. If it is impossible to get your leg to a 90-degree angle, some tightness is indicated. Ability to move the leg farther than 90 degrees would mean a good amount of flexibility in the muscles at the back of the hip (Figure 2.17). Tightness in the muscles at the front of the hip is demonstrated by lying on the stomach and lifting the leg directly to the back (Figure 2.18). The hips should remain on the floor while doing this action with the pelvis as level as possible.

Strength at the front of the hip can also be tested while lying on the back. Simply lift the leg above the body to a flexed position and continue to flex the hip while someone resists your movement (Figure 2.19). Roll to your stomach to test for strength at the back of the hip. This time hyperextend the hip against resistance (Figure 2.20). It might be interesting to test for strength both with and without outward rotation at the hip. Your partner can help you decide if you exert greater force in flexion or extension. You can investigate the degree of flexibility and strength in all other planes of action possible in the hip using this same method. Abduction, adduction, and inward and outward rotation can be judged as well.

Exercises to Improve Muscular Balance

The following series of exercises is provided to facilitate stretching and strengthening appropriate body areas to balance the body and produce better alignment. These suggestions are offered in pictorial form for clarity, but it is important to read the suggestions provided under each photograph. Figures 2.21a to 2.21t are exercises for stretching, whereas Figures 2.22a to 2.22n show ways to strengthen similar body areas (see pp. 68-71).

One of the ways to feel good alignment in your own body is to lie on the floor with your eyes closed. Feel the segments of the

a

b

c

Figure 2.17.   Leg lifted (a) 90 degrees to floor; (b) position indicates tight hamstrings; (c) position demonstrates flexibility in hamstrings.

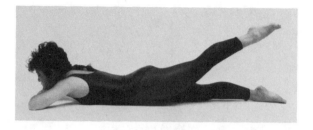

Figure 2.18.   Test for tightness at front of hip.

Figure 2.19.   Test for quadriceps strength (partner resists flexion at hip).

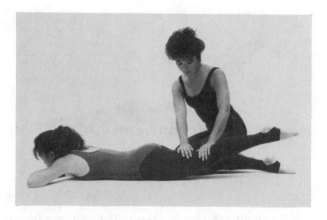

Figure 2.20.   Test for hamstrings strength through resistance.

body against the floor. Make no attempt to manipulate parts of your body into better alignment. Concentrate on your body in profile, and visualize a straight line running down your side just behind the ear, through the shoulder and hip, and a little in front of the ankle. See this line on both sides of your body as you stay with this image for awhile. Gradually come to sitting with legs crossed and wrists resting on your knees. Again visualize a line at the side of your body starting just behind the ear and running down through your hip into the floor. Experiment with rounding your back and then straightening to come back to good alignment. Notice differences in your body as you change positions. These feelings are a result of your body sense, also called *kinesthetic sense*.

Next go to standing, but keep your eyes closed. Be aware of the image of a straight line at your side when you arrive at your full height. Practice flexing and extending your spine again (Figure 2.23, p. 72). Notice differences in your kinesthetic sense as you change positions.

Concentrate on your feet once you have returned to a straight and aligned position. They should be flat on the floor with the big toe, little toe, and heel all touching the ground. This placement provides for a triangular distribution of weight throughout each foot (Penrod & Plastino, 1980). Make sure you are not rolling to the inner or outer borders of your feet (Figure 2.24).

Bring your mind back to the entire body, and in your mind's eye connect feet to head. Feel this connection throughout your entire body. Visualize your body growing taller so that your head reaches toward the ceiling, your neck lengthens, and your torso lifts out of your hips. Continue to feel your head above your shoulders and your shoulders above your torso and hips.

Centering

Centering is both a physical and a psychological concept. In the physical sense, it refers to the center of weight of a human body. The psychological aspect of centering has to do with feeling whole and grounded in the body.

Physical Center

The center of weight or gravity is the most dense portion of the body. It is located in the pelvis (Hawkins, 1964). The line dropping

Figure 2.21. Stretching exercises: (a) pectoral muscles; (b) another pectoral stretch; (c) sternum area; (d) abdominals; (e) hip flexors; (f) another stretch for hip flexors; (g) neck and upper back; (h) the back; (i) the back, particularly the lumbar area; (j) lower back, buttocks, and hamstrings; (k) hamstrings and buttocks (leave knee bent for safety); (l) more advanced hamstring stretch (do not hyperextend knee); (m) ab-

ductors; (n) another stretch for abductors; (o) adductors (inner thigh); (p) another adductor stretch; (q) back of lower leg; (r) also a stretch for calf; (s) hamstrings, quadriceps, and calf muscles; (t) back and lower leg area.

Figure 2.22. Strengthening exercises: (a) shoulder area (push-up from knees is less stressful); (b) push-up from elbows saves wrists; (c) push-up from feet and elbows; (d) abdominal muscles (to alleviate back stress, roll up only to position shown); (e) oblique abdominals; (f) quadriceps and other hip flexors; (g) also for hip flexors; (h) muscles in back; (i) hamstrings (move leg up and down, keeping toes pointing directly to the floor); (j) another strengthener for hamstrings; (k) abductors (maintain position with toes straight ahead); (l) adductors (alternately flex and ex-

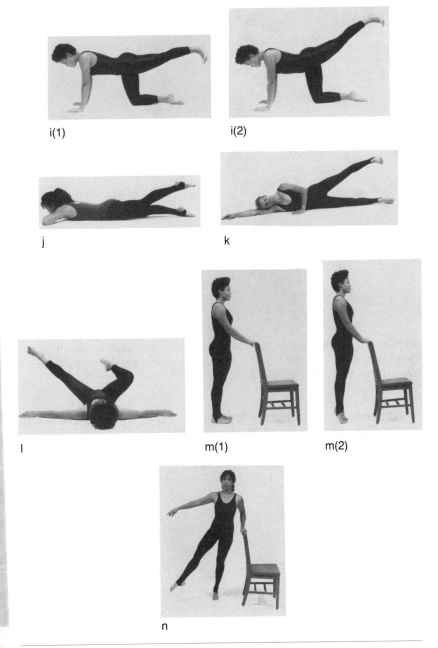

i(1)   i(2)

j   k

l   m(1)   m(2)

n

tend legs); (m) muscles at back of lower legs (lift and lower heel); (n) muscles at back of lower leg (lift and lower heel while standing on one foot).

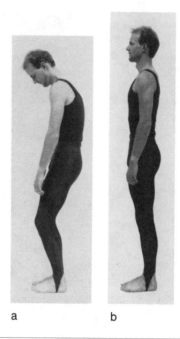

a   b

Figure 2.23.   Experiencing differences in body shape by moving from (a) rounded body shape, spine flexed to (b) straight alignment, spine extended (to be done with eyes closed).

vertically downward from the body's center to the center of the earth is the *line of gravity* (Hawkins, 1964). Its exact location can be calculated mathematically for each person by taking measurements from a photograph and inserting these measurements in a formula (Dempster, 1955). In reality, the center of weight is located in the pelvis slightly below the navel, with the female center being lower than that of the male.

Psychological Center

Some accounts of being centered say that it is to be lined up, solid, balanced, and right on—to operate on a feeling rather than a thinking level (Hendricks & Wills, 1975). Most people have had these sensations at times.

Explorations in Centering

One method of experiencing the body as whole and centered is to develop a heightened sense of energy flow. Isadora Duncan,

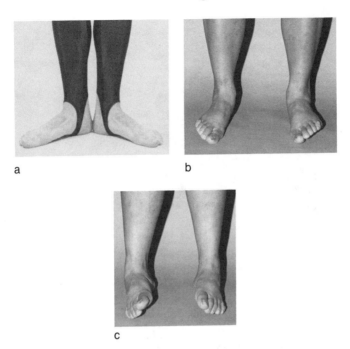

a   b

c

Figure 2.24. Weight distribution of foot: (a) evenly placed to form triangle, (b) carried on inner border, and (c) thrown to outside.

the famous dancer, often talked about the physical center and emotional center as one. She called this center the *solar plexis*. It is also possible to understand center as a place in the body from which energy flows out into the extremities.

You can gain a sense of this energy connection by sitting quietly on the floor with legs crossed and eyes closed. Feel the center of your body, and slowly let energy flow from center into one arm. The flow of energy will cause your arm to move to the side and away from center. Let the energy flow to your fingertips and beyond. The energy flow may take your body off to one side, but this is all right. Reverse this flow of energy so that your arm collapses to your side and the energy shrinks back to your center. Pick other parts of your body such as a leg or the head and neck, and allow energy to flow back and forth between center and those other body parts. Be conscious of differences in body feelings when energy is contained, when it is flowing outward, and when it shrinks back into the center. Continue with this exploration until energy flows and connects easily between center and each of the other parts of your body.

Stand quietly in one spot with your eyes closed and your feet under your shoulders. Decide how it feels to have your center

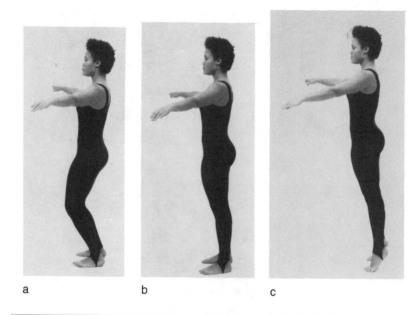

a   b   c

Figure 2.25.   Exploring difference in kinesthetic feeling at (a) low, (b) middle, and (c) high levels (concentrate on muscular feeling at each level).

over your feet. Flex your knees and extend them, keeping your center above your feet. Rise to the balls of your feet, and lift your center to come to this higher level. Continue this action, flexing, extending, and lifting. Motivate the action from your center, not from the feet or shoulders (Figure 2.25).

Open your eyes and walk forward slowly. As you transfer your weight from one foot to the other, be conscious of your center. While walking, think about moving your center forward rather than moving your feet. Keep your center over your feet with each step and let energy move out of your center. Your body should act as a whole instead of parts. Walk in other directions and remain aware of your center as you move; experience your body and its flow of energy as an integrated whole.

Hendricks and Wills have written *The Centering Book* (1975), in which they discuss the psychological aspects of centering. In one exploration called ear centering, they suggest closing the eyes and listening carefully to sounds outside, inside the room, and inside your ears. Hendricks and Wills believe that returning to this inner sound of the ears can be peaceful.

Gravity

Gravity is a constant force that acts upon the body. As long as you live upon planet Earth, gravity will act upon your body.

Gravity at Rest and During Movement

The line of gravity has already been discussed. It is a perpendicular line dropped down from the center of gravity to the floor. Gravity operates in standing alignment, but it is equally important in motion. In some kinds of movement, it is natural to resist the pull of gravity; in other actions, the pull of gravity helps propel the motion. When a person rises from a chair, the center of weight resists gravity's pull. If the individual gives in to gravity during the process, standing would never be achieved. On the other hand, we swing our arms when walking, and it is the pull of gravity that activates the downward part of the swing.

Explorations of Gravity

Sit down on the floor again in a cross-legged position. Close your eyes. Gently lift one arm away from the floor. Feel how gravity pulls down on all arm segments. Slowly give in to gravity and let your arm go back toward the floor. Lift your arm again, but this time give in quickly to the downward pull. Try lifting and releasing other parts of your body.

Gradually come to standing. As you rise, feel how the center of your body must pull away from the earth. Stretch as high as you can, and then collapse gradually back to the floor. Repeat this lifting and lowering action. Then open your eyes and rapidly collapse.

Maintain a standing position, and concentrate on one arm. Swing this arm back and forth at the side of your body. As you swing your arm, notice that energy is required to lift your arm, but that gravity takes over on the downward part of the swing. If you do not release on the downward part of this action, you are not performing a true swing. Practice swinging other parts of your body like the head, neck, or a leg. You can also do a swing with the whole upper part of the body by using the waist as the point from which the swing occurs.

Walk forward again. The swinging action of both the arms and legs is an integral part of each step. See if you can feel the application of energy and the release into gravity of each leg swing as you move. Next vary your use of energy as you walk. Experiment using a lot of energy and then very little to initiate each step. During each stride, try changing the point at which you apply energy. Decide how these changes alter your customary walking style.

Balance

Balance is a precarious and wonderful thing. It is exciting when achieved, but frustrating when lost. Any dance student can give you many examples of problems in balance.

Base of Support

The most stable position is lying flat on the floor. Decreasing contact with the floor reduces stability and makes balance more difficult. A larger base of support provides for stability; a smaller base makes the body less secure (Hinson, 1977). Figure 2.26 shows positions in which the base of support becomes smaller.

Center of Gravity

The level of the center of gravity also affects balancing ability. The lower the center, the more stable the body (Hinson, 1977). This is why it is a natural reaction to put the feet wide apart and lower the center to stop rapid motion. Broadening the base and lowering the center both increase stability and reduce continuation of momentum (Figure 2.27).

Another factor that influences balance is the location of your center. Balance is maintained more easily when the center of weight is above the base. Shifting the center away from this position disturbs good alignment and makes balancing difficult.

Explorations of Balance

Stand with your heels together and your eyes closed. Picture the alignment of your whole body and feel your feet against the floor. You may find your weight shifting from foot to foot as you stand.

a

b

c

Figure 2.26. Differences in stability: (a) very secure position, (b) fairly stable with wide base, and (c) less stable due to decrease in size of base.

Figure 2.27. A technique for stopping with wide base and lower center.

Figure 2.28. Experience postural sway by shifting weight from one foot to the other.

This is the natural postural swaying of your body (Figure 2.28). Let this swaying increase slightly and tune into the various feelings of tension and relaxation as they occur. Try swaying in directions other than side to side. Open your eyes and continue swaying. Gradually let the swaying get larger, so that you finally go off balance (J. Aston, personal communication, summer, 1983 [class notes]). Fall, move in a direction, and recover your balance by bringing your center above your feet.

After you have experimented with balance on two feet, shift your weight while balancing on one foot. Bring your center above your base, and then test how far your upper body can go to the side beyond your base before you must fall (Hawkins, 1964; Figure 2.29).

It is fun to test your balance by decreasing the size of your base. Stand on one foot with your center right over your foot. Place the fingertips of one hand on a chair or wall, and lift your heel off the floor. Lift and lower the heel several times. Stay in the raised position, take your hand off the wall, and continue to balance in the lifted position (Figure 2.30). Balance is maintained more readily by lifting the center of gravity and keeping it over your supporting foot. Picture this center-to-foot connection in your mind.

You can improve your ability to balance by working with the body's energy flow. Remember that energy flows from the body's center. Stand with your feet apart under your shoulders; lift your heels off the floor, and extend your arms to the side at shoulder level (Figure 2.31). Feel energy radiating out into the arms and legs from the center. Use this flow of energy to help balance your body. In effective balance, energy flows into one part of the body to counterbalance energy flow into other body parts. If too much energy flows into one arm, you should be able to pull some of it back and channel it into the other arm or leg. This basic principle is known as *balance and compensation*. Whenever one part

a   b

Figure 2.29.   Balance on one foot: (a) keep center over base; (b) shifting center away from base makes balance more precarious.

Figure 2.30.   In balancing with small base, keep center over base.

Figure 2.31.   Balance is improved by directing energy out from center into arms, legs, and neck.

of the body moves away from the line of gravity, an opposing part must move in an opposite direction to counterbalance the body (Hawkins, 1964; Figure 2.32).

You can explore balance and compensation by placing the body in many different positions. In each of these, practice connecting center to extremities. Stand with the heels together, and sway from side to side. As your hips go to one side let your upper body reach in the opposite direction (Figure 2.33). Feel the connection between upper and lower body halves, and decide how much you

Figure 2.32. Counterbalance by equalizing energy flow in different directions.

Figure 2.33. Counterbalancing energy between arms and opposite hip.

must reach with the arms and upper body to compensate for the opposite pull in the hips.

A body position in which the right side visually matches the left is symmetrical (Figure 2.34). Symmetrical body shapes appear balanced to the eye. In asymmetrical positions, the body is

Figure 2.34. Symmetrical body shape.

Figure 2.35. Asymmetrical body position.

not visually balanced; more of the body's mass appears to be on the right or left side (Humphrey, 1959; Figure 2.35). Assume a symmetrical position followed by an asymmetrical one. The two types of body shape should feel different to you. Practice some variations on symmetrical and asymmetrical shaping. Be aware of the channeling of energy between center and extremities. Work at balancing in the different shapes by playing with the body's energy flow. When too much energy goes in one direction, let some of it flow back through center into another part of the body to compensate and thus counterbalance your body.

Breathing

Proper breathing is energizing and relaxing. In fact, breathing has been called the interface between mind and body (I. Dowd, personal communication, summer, 1981 [class notes]). Many people go through life, however, without breathing fully and deeply, existing on shallow and inefficient amounts of air.

Dancers frequently talk about breathing with movement. They believe that proper breathing during movement adds vitality to a performance. It helps movement come alive and project to an audience. In general, dancers breathe in to suspend movement and out when they give in to the pull of gravity (Humphrey, 1959). Dancers talk about taking breath into parts of the body as a technique of energizing an area. They believe that each movement must be filled with breath to be alive (Hawkins, 1964).

Explorations at Rest

Lie down on the floor and close your eyes. Tune into your natural breath pattern, being sensitive to the constant rhythm of inhaling and exhaling. Continue to tune into your breathing; you should find this involvement in your breathing relaxing. (Note: Some of the explorations in this and other chapters are done lying on the floor. Some people may need a mat or pad for the body. If your hips, shoulders, or elbows dig into the floor, use a mat or even a towel or blanket to cushion body parts.)

The direction of your breathing can be altered by emphasizing either vertical or horizontal directions (P. Hanstein, personal communication, summer, 1980 [class notes]). Still lying on the floor, attempt to breathe in a vertical direction from head to toes, with each breath going to the pelvic floor. Change your breathing to the horizontal direction. Placing your hands on either side of your rib cage will help accentuate the horizontal nature of your breath because you will feel how your ribs expand to the side and contract toward the midline of your body. Be sure to take a rest from this exaggerated breathing because it can cause dizziness.

Focus on your breathing again, and this time try to empty your lungs completely as you exhale. It helps to picture your lungs as two sacs or balloons, one on each side of your chest. Visualize these two sacs being completely deflated on exhalation and filling completely with inhalation. Contraction of the abdominal muscles also helps to force air out of the lungs.

Explorations During Movement

Bend down near the floor and close your eyes. As you do so, breathe in and let your body ascend slowly until you come to standing. Return to your original position, breathing out as you descend. Repeat this sequence of actions. Up to this point your breathing should have been smooth or even. Now as you ascend and descend, breathe in and out in spurts of air. What is the difference between these two methods of breathing, and how does a change in breathing style affect movement quality?

Stand with your feet apart and eyes closed. Direct your breath into one part of your body and then into another. As you breathe into a part of the body let it expand, grow, and move. Start with small actions and gradually change to larger motions.

Stand with feet slightly apart and toes straight ahead. Lift both arms to an overhead position. As you swing the arms down to your sides, exhale and let the upper body curve forward. Follow this action by bringing the arms back to the original pose, uncurling the upper body and breathing in (Figure 2.36). A varia-

a   b   c

Figure 2.36. Sequence of actions using breathing pattern: (a) assume starting position; (b) flex spine, swinging arms down and breathing out, and (c) extend spine while breathing in.

tion on the preceding exercise begins with both arms at your sides. From this position, move the upper body at the waist to the side, front, other side, and back and then return to center. You should trace a circular pathway in space with the upper body. Accompany the body circling with breath out on the downward part of the sequence and breathe in as you circle up. Let your head and neck relax and go with the movement of the body (Figure 2.37).

A leg lift or kick is another way to connect moving and breathing. Stand with weight on both feet and arms in abduction at your sides. Lift one leg directly in front of your body to a comfortable height and breathe into it at the same time. You should be able to take your breath into this leg and release it beyond your toes (Figure 2.38).

Go back to a position with weight on both feet and heels together. Let your arms hang loosely at your sides. Push against the floor and lift your heels. When you come down from this position, bend your knees. Repeat this action, breathing in as you push up and out as you come down to the flexed-knee position (Figure 2.39). If your legs feel solid beneath you, carry the action into a series of small jumps. During the pattern of this action you flex the leg joints to push off and land; inhale as you push off for the jump, and exhale to land. Decide whether breathing with your jump helps you to go higher in the air (Figure 2.40).

Devise an original sequence of actions. Practice this sequence, and see where you need to inhale and where exhaling seems more appropriate. Be sure that your breath pattern helps your movement.

The person in Figure 2.41 is demonstrating a longer series of actions. Execute this pattern by moving smoothly from one body shape to the next. Find where you need to inhale and exhale in this pattern. Do not hold your breath.

As you progress through each day, remember to breathe. When you feel tense take some extra deep, cleansing breaths. If you take an exercise class or participate in some kind of exercise on your own, learn to breathe with the phrasing of the movement.

Tension and Relaxation

Many people go through life holding excessive tension in their bodies. Usually these individuals do not realize the amount of tension they carry around until they have a chance to relax. *Aston Patterning* is a body therapy system in which the goal is

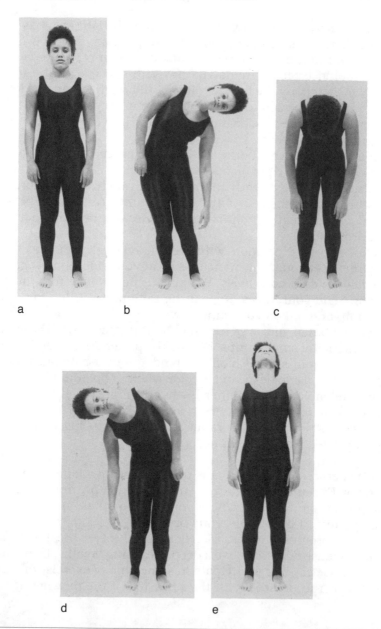

a   b   c

d   e

Figure 2.37. Explore moving and breathing: (a) assume starting position; (b) flex spine laterally and begin to exhale; (c) move into forward, flexed position and continue to exhale; (d) take body to laterally flexed position on other side and begin to inhale; and (e) go to place with upper spine hyperextended while completing inhaling phase (move smoothly between poses).

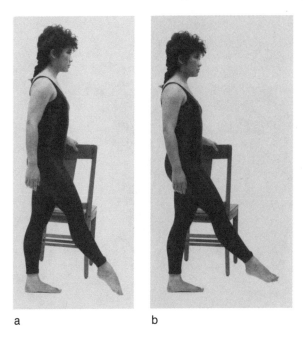

a   b

Figure 2.38.   Practice breathing into foot and toes: (a) correct position with toes extended; (b) incorrect position with toes flexed or relaxed.

finding and releasing habitual tension patterns. Judith Aston (personal communication, summer, 1983 [class notes]) believes that stresses are held in the body where they inhibit natural energy flow. Painful or stressful situations become locked into the body in the form of tension patterns called *holding patterns*.

In the book *Gestalt Therapy*, Perls, Hefferline, and Goodman (1951) talk about such patterns of tension. They also work with developing a heightened awareness of these tensions and connect them to emotional content. The suggestion is that if you mobilize some particular pattern such as a tightened jaw, it tends to arouse a dim emotion. Conversely, in the presence of frustrating circumstances you usually do not feel an emotion until you accept the corresponding body actions as your own. Emotions associated with experiences are felt in the body where they create the tension patterns. These patterns, in turn, are held in muscles until released through exercise or other methods.

Stress

Think about your own daily experiences, and try to remember one that was particularly stressful. Remember how you felt at

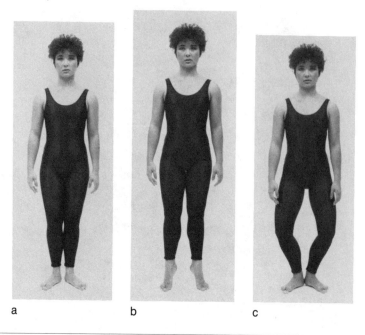

a   b   c

Figure 2.39. Raising and lowering body: (a) assume starting position; (b) lift to balance on balls of feet, breathe in; and (c) lower to flat feet with knees bent, breathe out.

a   b

Figure 2.40. Jumping and breathing: (a) begin by flexing knees, and (b) inhale and push off (exhaling takes place while returning to the floor).

Figure 2.41. More complex movement pattern: (a) assume starting pose, (b) reach up and to side, (c) go to low lunge, (d) lift higher and move to other side, and (e) start to lift off floor (connect poses with continuous movement, breathing out while moving down and in while moving up).

the end of this day. You were tired, tense, and in no mood to be around people. Your main desire was to go home and relax. You can probably also recall body feelings that accompanied the stress—a tight lower back, tense shoulders, or a rigid neck. Be sensitive to how your body responds the next time you are upset, tense, or tired.

It is impossible to escape stress and strain unless you want to live in an insulated world without work or contact with other people. Such a world is boring, and so the challenge is to learn how to deal effectively with daily stress.

One remedy for stress is to participate in some form of exercise each day. Exercising brings you back to the body level where you are required to do instead of think. You focus on movement instead of your problems. To encourage regular participation in exercise, choose a form that appeals to you—one that you feel good about.

Another way to reduce stress is to practice some relaxation exercises each day. These exercises could include meditation, deep breathing, or any of the other ideas suggested in this book. Appropriate music can also help set the mood.

Explorations in Relaxation

The position in Figure 2.42 encourages physical relaxation. It is called *constructive rest* and was devised by kinesiologist Lulu Sweigard. In this position the pull of gravity aids reduction of muscle tension, taking stress off the joints by placing them in a flexed position (Sweigard, 1974). In constructive rest, the back and feet rest on the floor with the arms folded across the body. Some individuals find it more comfortable to let the arms rest at their sides.

Assume the constructive rest position (Figure 2.42) or any other position you find relaxing. Find the points of tension in your body;

Figure 2.42.   Constructive rest position.

emphasize your breathing and see if you can breathe into the tense areas (I. Dowd, personal communication, summer, 1981 [class notes]).

You can work with a partner to discover points of retained tension in your body. Lie down, but this time do not flex the leg joints. Close your eyes and allow your partner to lift one of your arms a little off the floor by holding your hand. Next let your partner move your arm up, down, and sideways (Figure 2.43). Your arm should remain limp throughout this test. Do not assist or resist the moving of your arm, but give its full weight to your partner. There may be resistance where your arm cannot be

a

b

Figure 2.43. Test for tension: (a) gently hold hand of person and (b) move arm around (resistance of body part being moved indicates tension).

moved as easily. These places of resistance indicate points where you hold tension. Test the other arm and both legs using the same method (J. Aston, personal communication, summer, 1983 [class notes]).

Visual images can also aid relaxation. The goal is to paint a picture in your mind that is associated with a relaxed state. When using visual imagery, you need to paint a clear picture—one in which you can get involved. Some examples of relaxing images follow.

Imagine yourself lying on a warm feather bed; feel the parts of your body sinking into the feather bed as it caresses your body. See yourself relaxing on a beautiful beach on a summer day. You can hear the waves in the background and the leaves gently rustling in the wind. You feel cool, calm, and relaxed. A third image is that of floating with the whole body hovering above the floor just like a cloud floating in the sky.

Another image combines breathing and visualization for purposes of relaxation. Take several slow and very deep breaths from the abdomen. With each inhalation imagine yourself taking in energy from the universe. Let the body relax, and visualize the inside of the body as growing more radiant outward from the center (Samuels & Bennett, 1973).

Jacobson's *progressive relaxation* is one of the most established of relaxation techniques. The point of this system is to teach people how to differentiate a tense body from one that is relaxed; a sensitivity to tension is developed by focusing on it and then releasing it.

Lie down on the floor and close your eyes to begin the relaxation sequence. Leave your arms at your side and your legs straight. Allow your arms and legs to rotate outward. Begin with your right arm and make it as tight and tense as you can. Your shoulder and elbow are tight and your hand is in a fist. Now gradually release tension in your arm. Start with the fingers, feeling a wave of relaxation flow from hand to shoulder. Practice tensing and relaxing your right arm until you are confident about controlling the two kinesthetic feelings and differentiating between them. Do the same sequence in the other extremities. Take the body parts—left arm, right leg, and left leg—and tense and relax them one at a time. Finally, tense and gradually relax your entire body. When you tense your whole body, all your joints are rigid, your back is pressed to the floor, and your neck is tight. Begin at the outside of your body and slowly release. The head and neck, hands, and feet relax first, and the sense of ease slowly creeps toward center (Jacobson, 1929). Take time to contrast the kinesthetic feelings found in these two states—tension and relaxation.

Chapter Three

Analyzing Movement

Habitual tension patterns and postures of the body were discussed in chapter 2. It should follow that if people hold the body in specific ways, set and sometimes ineffective movement patterns can evolve. In this chapter you will be looking at some of the actions you do each day. In fact, you probably take these movements for granted, because they are such an integral part of your daily routine. The human body becomes the center of focus only when individuals are injured, and thus have problems with common tasks. At this point, one realizes that the body is a marvelous instrument—one that serves well and asks for very little in return.

Mechanical Efficiency
in Common Movement

We perform many kinds of movement, such as sitting down, carrying, and lifting. Performing these actions in the best way, however, means learning more about the mechanical efficiency of each.

Sitting Down

The proper way for you to sit involves bringing the back of one leg close to or touching the chair; your other leg is farther forward and carries the weight (Figure 3.1). Your center of gravity is then lowered straight down while keeping the shoulders above the hips as much as possible. Your body will incline forward slightly as the weight is transferred to the rear foot. Do not drop your weight abruptly into a chair. When sitting, try not to reach back with the hips first. This action leaves the head out in front of the pelvis and puts strain on the back.

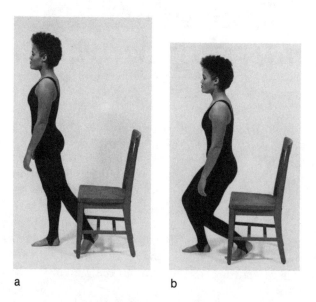

a   b

Figure 3.1.   Sitting down: (a) to begin, extend one leg behind body; (b) keep head above shoulders as much as possible.

Standing Up

When standing up from a seated position, let the leg extensor muscles do their work. Place one foot in front of the other, and, keeping the head and body in line, incline the trunk forward, pushing off from the back foot (Figure 3.2); in the process of standing the weight is transferred to the front foot (Lee & Wagner, 1949). Have someone watch you sit and stand. Be aware of the location of your center when performing these actions; it may help to have a feeling of lifting your center out of the hips when you sit and stand.

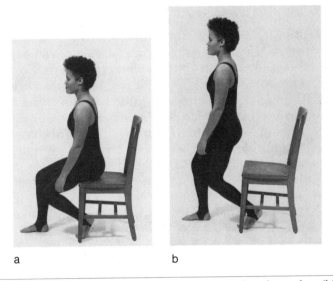

a   b

Figure 3.2.   Standing: (a) to begin, reach forward with one leg; (b) maintain good alignment during standing.

Sitting

Once you are seated other situations arise. You may find that all chairs are not equally suitable for your body. Some cause you to lean too far back; others are too high or too low. Try out a chair before buying it. If you plan to use a chair for work at a desk, sit in it and practice writing on a surface similar in height to the one you will be using.

It is very hard on the shoulders and upper back if a chair is too low. You should be able to sit and do your work without hunching the shoulders. Chairs that are too high are also un-comfortable because feet hang in the air rather than resting comfortably on the floor. Check to see whether chairs you already own can be adjusted; if the level of the seat cannot be changed, sit on a cushion if the chair is too low. Seat height behind the steering wheel in your car is also important. Constant lifting of your shoulders while holding the steering wheel can cause acute cramping in the upper back. Many people spend a lot of time in a car, and the comfort and convenience of the driver's seat must be taken into consideration.

Walking

Many people think that walking involves the legs and feet alone. In truth, it includes placement and use of the entire body. Good alignment is essential to an efficient walking pattern. Remember that there should be a straight line at the side of the body down through the foot. It is also important that this line of posture not tilt too far forward or backward during locomotion and not break at the head, shoulders, or hips (Figure 2.7). Front and back views can provide additional information concerning an individual's walking pattern. From these two views it is possible to see if the person puts greater weight on one foot or the other, if the shoulders and hips are level, and if both arms swing with equal intensity (M. Myers, personal communication, summer, 1987 [class notes]).

The pattern of wear on shoes can tell you a lot about weight placement during each step. Excessive wear on the heels indicates that weight is carried too far back. Wear at the front of the soles is produced by a forward lean, and when the outside of the heel is worn down weight is thrown to the outside. The height of heel on a shoe also affects weight bearing, because higher heels cause body alignment to tip farther forward. Negative heel shoes (those with heels that are lower at the back) have an opposite effect.

Have a partner watch you walk, looking at all three views of the body—front, side, and back. As you walk, feel your center of weight lifting out of your hips. This correction will make you lighter on your feet and will prevent you from dropping your weight into either hip as you transfer it from foot to foot.

Some kinds of misalignments such as forward shoulders or a protruding abdomen can be lessened through the balancing exercises described in chapter 2. A forward or backward lean can also be changed by consciously adjusting your stance. If you find that you lean in one direction or the other, stand still and reposition your head and shoulders. Have your partner help you with these postural changes, and then walk using this new orientation. Be patient. Changes in alignment feel strange at first, because you may be accustomed to doing the wrong thing. Concentration on the image of a straight line at the side of your body may help.

Go back to the front and back views of your body. Walk for your partner, and see if you are able to place your weight in the same way on each foot and to swing your arms evenly with each step. Decide what the new uses of your arms and legs feel like kinesthetically in your body, so that you can duplicate these changes each time you walk. If you roll to the inside or outside of your feet, you may need lifts in your shoes. Consult a podiatrist about the placement and size of lifts.

Walking is a more complex locomotor pattern than many expect until they have had a chance to analyze it. It is fun and interesting to watch people walk. Pick any public place in which you can sit and observe. You will see many variations on the walking theme. Learn to focus on your own body and its movements.

Climbing Stairs

Climbing stairs takes walking into different terrain. The individual is again viewed from front, side, and back. Placement of weight and lift in the center can be judged from front and back. The side view allows you to judge arm swing and alignment from head to toe. One of the common problems in climbing is to lean the body too far forward. Climbing is more efficient with the center lifted and the head carried as directly above the hips as possible (Figure 3.3a). Incline the entire body forward to assist in the weight shift as you climb, but avoid extending the body too far forward, as this can cause back strain (Figure 3.3b). This inclination should include the whole body from the ankles up. Plant the whole foot on the step above, extend the knee and hip, and swing the lower leg forward to the next step (Lee & Wagner, 1949). Place the whole foot on each step, not just the ball of the foot (Figure 3.3c), and use handrails to aid balance, not to support you. Practice going up and down a stairway several times. Be aware of your alignment as you do this. If you are a hiker, try incorporating some of the above suggestions into your uphill technique.

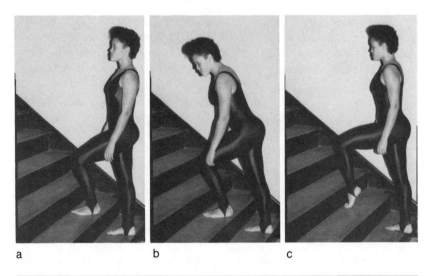

a   b   c

Figure 3.3. Climbing stairs: (a) keep head above shoulders; (b) carrying head in front of shoulder can cause back strain; (c) plant the whole foot on each step, not the ball of the foot.

Lifting

Lifting is another activity performed on a daily basis. One of the rules to remember is to bend down near the object to be lifted, and then return to standing keeping the object near your center of gravity (Figures 3.4a and b). The amount of flexion in your hips and knees should be in relation to the weight of the object to be lifted. The heavier the weight, the deeper the flexion that is needed. Keep your weight distributed between both feet as you lift and mentally prepare your muscles for the load. Do not flex the hips and lift an object with the back straight or extended and the load held away from the body (Figures 3.4c and d). Back strain could result because too much of the body is extended out in front of the center of gravity. When possible, divide heavy loads to be lifted (Lee & Wagner, 1949; Figure 3.5).

Carrying

While carrying a load, keep it as close to the body as possible and over your base (Figure 3.6). Shift a load from side to side, and extend an arm in the opposite direction to counterbalance the object or objects being carried in a single load (Figure 3.7). When possible try not to hold a load directly in front of your body (Lee & Wagner, 1949).

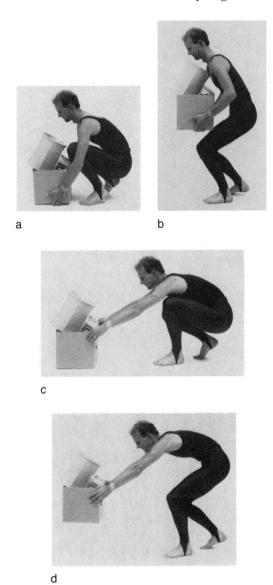

Figure 3.4. Lifting: (a) bend down close to object; (b) continue action, keeping object close to body's center; (c) an example of incorrect lifting technique; (d) object is held too far from center throughout action.

Have a partner observe you lifting and carrying a medium-weight object. Keep your head and shoulders above your hips and the object near your center throughout the action. Think of some other daily activities and subject them to the same type of analysis.

Figure 3.5.   Divide a load, carrying it equally on both sides of the body.

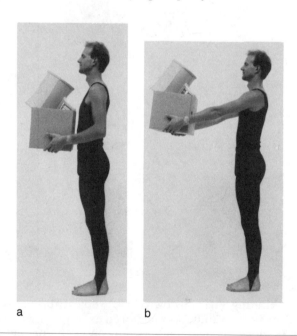

a   b

Figure 3.6.   Holding load: (a) correct position with object close to center and (b) incorrect position.

Elements of Movement

For many years, dancers, and particularly dance educators, have been using a method of movement analysis based on the ele-

Figure 3.7. Counterbalance one-sided load by extending arm in opposite direction.

ments of movement—space, time, and energy. This method of analysis has become an essential part of dance education methods used in teaching both movement skills and composition or choreography.

Space

Space, the first category of movement analysis, refers to the way individuals move body parts in the surrounding space, or the way in which they travel across space. All movement occurs in space or takes up space. The spatial category, in turn, has a number of subareas that aid in making accurate movement descriptions. Dance educators say that actions can occur in a number of *directions* such as forward, backward, or to either side, right or left (Minton, 1984). In addition, there are the diagonal directions to the right and left in front of the body and to the right and left behind an individual. An important point here is that direction can refer to (a) the direction in which the body faces, (b) the direction in which body parts reach in relation to the body's center, or (c) the direction in which the whole body is moved across space. Figure 3.8 shows the person facing in a forward direction, whereas in Figure 3.9 all individuals are facing backward. Body facing could also be into side or diagonal directions (Figures 3.10 and 3.11). The two dancers in Figure 3.12 are reaching in opposite directions—one to the right and the other to the left of the

Figure 3.8.   Facing forward.

Figure 3.9.   Facing backward.

center of their bodies. In contrast, the individual in Figure 3.13 is performing an arm circle in which her arm moves through both forward and backward directions in relation to her center. Reaching or stretching of body parts could also enter any of the four diagonals described earlier. Finally, one could move the whole body across space in any of these eight directions.

Figure 3.10. Facing to the side.

Figure 3.11. Reaching to diagonal.

To experience these various directions, move your body forward, to the side, backward, and to the various diagonals. Be aware of how it feels to move and change directions. Moving forward will probably be most comfortable for you, whereas going

Figure 3.12. Reaching in opposite directions.

Figure 3.13. Arm circle travels through front and back directions (in relation to center of body).

backward may make you a little uneasy. Experiment to see if you can change directions within a certain number of counts. Go sideways, for example, for eight counts, and then change to movement to the back or to a diagonal for eight more counts. Try not to stop in order to make these directional changes, but see if you can perform each transition smoothly and quickly.

Size of movement is also an essential aspect of the movement element space. It can vary from extremely large to very small. Pick a movement such as the gesture of waving or saluting, and see how large you can make this gesture. Gradually decrease the size of your action until you are performing as small a movement as possible. Notice the differences in energy and tension that are required for executing large and small movements.

Another aspect of use of space is *level* (Minton, 1984). Movement level can be high, middle, or low, or at any level in between these three. Middle level movement is where human locomotion normally takes place. When we walk or run we customarily do so at a middle level; jumping or moving on half toe on the balls of the feet takes the body into actions at a high level. Moving at low level is to move closer to the floor with the knees bent in some degree of flexion.

Two final aspects of the element space are *focus* and *pathway*. Focus refers to the point at which the face and/or eyes are directed. Pathway is the line traced by one or more body parts in space as movement occurs (Minton, 1984). Pathway can vary from curved or rounded to straight lines.

Reach for an object such as a pan or potted plant. Your spatial pathway was probably a straight line to the goal object; it would be wasted effort to pick up these objects using a curved-line pattern. Think of tasks for which a curved spatial pattern is more appropriate, and try them. Also take note of where in space your focus is directed in each of these actions (Figure 3.14). A tennis

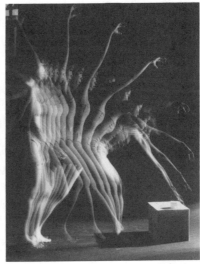

a   b

Figure 3.14. The pathway of hand to object can be (a) relatively straight or (b) curved.

forehand, an underhand toss, and the kick in football all use a curved line in space as traced by the part of the body executing the action.

Time

A second element of movement analysis is *time*. It can be fast or slow, or fall anywhere between these two extremes. The speed at which a task is performed can alter its effectiveness to a great degree. Probably the greatest problem with use of time is to believe that quick movement always increases efficiency, when a slower action could be more beneficial. This situation can be compared to the age-old saying of haste makes waste. In other words, there is a right and a wrong speed for each action.

Practice walking very slowly. You should discover that the transfer of weight from one foot to the other seems precarious and that this slow speed interrupts the natural rhythm of your arm swing. Gradually increase the speed of your walk until you find a tempo that feels natural. Then increase your walking speed to a point at which you are moving as fast as possible. Such a fast walk is hard to maintain because it takes so much added energy and seems disjointed and out of rhythm.

Watch others walk. You will see that some people saunter, and some are comfortable with a more lively pace. Individuals acquire their typical walking speed and style through life experiences so that a comfortable speed becomes habit. As your observation abilities become better developed, you will find many fascinating variations on the walking theme.

Energy

Energy, or *force*, is the third and final element of movement. Energy propels movement. It is the force that makes an action happen. When dance educators discuss the use of energy accompanying a movement, they frequently speak about quality as a method of describing energy use.

Qualities. The six basic *qualities* are sustained, percussive, vibratory, swinging, suspension, and collapse (Minton, 1984). *Sustained* movement is slow, controlled, and smooth. It looks like a performer in a slow-motion film. Actions done in a *percussive* manner make straight lines in space and have an explosive application of energy. Many of the movements of karate are percussive. *Vibratory* actions are done with a shaking or trembling quality in a single body part, or in the whole body, while swinging motions trace a curved line or an arc in space. In *swinging*, it is especially important to give in to gravity, or relax on the downward part of the motion, and then to apply energy on the upward portion of the arc. If energy is not used in this way, swinging is transformed into sustained movement.

Suspension and *collapse* are the last two of the energy qualities. In suspension the body or the part of the body being suspended has a feeling of hovering above the ground. This hovering action, for example, is common at the highest point in a leap, giving the individual the sensation of being suspended above the earth. A collapse is opposite in quality to that of a suspended movement. Here the feeling is one of giving into gravity and of moving toward the earth. A collapsing action can be done in either a fast or a slow manner. See if you can think of some daily activities in which a collapsing energy quality is appropriate.

Analysis.   All of the elements of movement can be applied to two diverse areas of study. They can be used to analyze daily actions (a) for the purpose of increasing efficiency, and (b) for understanding the emotional impact of human gesture on the observer. When employed for the first purpose—increased effectiveness of movement—the elements can be used to analyze tasks performed by various kinds of workers to eliminate wasted motion and increase efficiency.

Pick an activity you do each day. It could be typing, getting into your car, opening a door, or any other common movement sequence that is part of your life. Analyze your choice of space, time, and energy throughout the sequence. (This exercise might be easier to do with a partner.) Write down the conclusions of your analysis in the categories of space, time, and energy and decide whether a change in any of these categories would improve performance of the task. Be precise in your evaluation.

If you prefer, select a sequence of actions in a sport skill as the basis of your analysis. The movement pattern could be a tennis serve, a volleyball spike, or the swing of a baseball bat. Again, apply all categories of analysis to the action, deciding where changes, if any, should be made. Practice the sport pattern incorporating the changes, so your body gets accustomed to the new methods. Be sensitive to kinesthetic feelings that accompany any changes, because doing so will enable you to retain improvements in muscular memory. Figure 3.15 shows the spatial pathway of two actions—one from dance and one from sports.

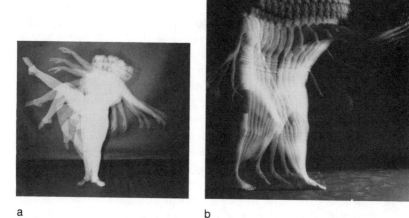

a   b

Figure 3.15. Curved spatial pathways traced by (a) leg and foot and
(b) arm and hand.

An example of a space, time, and energy analysis follows. A
forehand lob in tennis is an action familiar to most people. Furthermore, it is also a large action and easy to see. If it is performed
effectively, the use of space for the arm goes through the pathway
of an arc from a position slightly behind to a point on a diagonal
in front of the body. At the same time, level changes occur from
low, to middle, and then to a higher level during the follow-
through. The individual's focus should, of course, be on the ball.
Body facing changes from side to front, and the weight of the entire body shifts in a forward direction from the back to the front
foot. Timing of the tennis forehand is fast, and the use of energy
quality is somewhat percussive.

Nonverbal Aspects of Movement

A shrug of the shoulders goes with being unsure, a handshake
is a friendly greeting, and the hand held in front of the body with
palm forward indicates stop. Such gestures are established in
Western society, because they have certain meanings for those
with the same cultural orientation. The spoken word is not necessary for recognition of such gestural messages.

Nonverbal Connections

A natural connection exists between the verbal and the non-verbal. One might argue that the body communicates on another level—one that is totally different from verbal expression. Some authorities, however, believe that all verbal communication is accompanied by constant shifts in the body; changes in the meaning of the spoken word are connected to alterations of posture and gesture. The following experiment has to do with this verbal/nonverbal connection.

Concentrate on a word, particularly one that has a feeling state associated with it. *Happy* is such a word. Say the word *happy*, and then make an appropriate gesture to go with the word. This gesture could be uplifted arms, a wave, or a friendly smile. Say *happy* again, and attempt to simultaneously perform a gesture that is opposite in meaning. You will find that this is very difficult, and probably impossible, to do, because it goes against the natural mind/body connection.

Rugg (1963) studied the mind/body connection within the context of creative work. He found that writers and artists needed a certain environment to work effectively. Both body and mind require a specific atmosphere to encourage productive work. The whole person thinks and creates; everything we do is through the body, and not just in the mind. Rugg also discovered that the struggle for self-expression was accompanied by body feelings that came before any kind of creative work was realized. The tensile strength of the body is important to the creative act. Rugg called this tensing of the body *felt-thought*: a motor adjustment of the body that acts as a sounding board in responding to the world.

François Delsarte was a French music teacher during the nineteenth century. One of his goals was to describe the connection between feeling state and gesture. After observing many people, Delsarte decided that specific use of posture or gesture communicated feelings that could be read and experienced by the observer.

One of Delsarte's first ideas was to understand the human being as three persons combined in unity. These three principles were life, soul, and mind (Delsarte, 1887). In addition, Delsarte devised a codified system of gestures and postures through which any part of the body could communicate meaning by being placed in a certain position. Gesture was the method of interpreting sentiment (Delsarte). The hand with fingers apart meant exaltation, and with fingers dropped down abandon (Zorn, 1968; Figures 3.16a and b). To cross one leg in front of the other leaving only the toes of the back leg on the floor indicated ceremony, with the heel of the front foot at the arch of the back foot showed strength or independence, and with one foot behind and away from the other foot communicated terror (Zorn; Figures 3.16c, d, and e). Figures 3.16f through h, demonstrate some other poses that Delsarte believed communicated a specific message.

Delsarte's system of gestural and postural communication appears rigid today, but it was an early attempt to make the organic connection between body and expression a visible reality. Many people have used Delsarte's ideas, and today his work is a part of basic studies in dance, pantomime, and drama.

Elements of Movement and the Nonverbal

Analysis by means of the elements of movement can be used to understand nonverbal communication or body language. Variation in use of space, time, and energy alters the efficiency of an action and affects the communication aspect of movement at the same time. Considering each of the elements of movement one at a time will help you understand how we communicate nonverbally through movement.

Remember that the spatial factor of an action can vary in terms of direction, size, level, focus, and pathway. To the observer, changes in each of these aspects of space have differing emotional impacts. For example, according to Humphrey (1959), movement straight forward has power, whereas to go backward provides a diminishing effect, because the body of the individual performing the action appears to grow smaller in size. She believed that movement at a high level with focus directed upward and outward has a sense of elation and excitement; low level action with focus downward appears somber or dejected. Straight lines or pathways in space are more forceful than are the lyrical and graceful feeling of a curved-line path (Figure 3.17).

In the same sense we can say that slow use of time is calm and lethargic; it has a much softer feeling about it than quick time. In terms of energy, sustained quality also has a slow feeling about it. Percussive use of energy is powerful, strong, and explosive; vibratory nervous and weak; and swinging relaxed and joyful. See if you can decide what the energy qualities of suspension and collapse represent for you.

The connection between changes in the elements of movement and the projected meaning should gradually become clear to you.

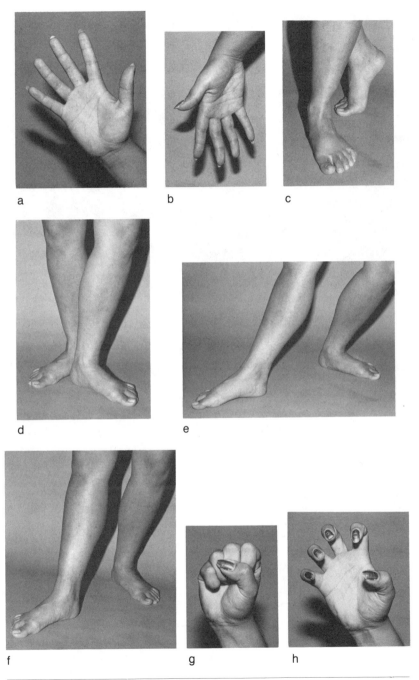

Figure 3.16. Delsarte gestures said to communicate (a) exaltation, (b) abandon, (c) ceremony, (d) strength/independence, (e) terror, (f) hesitation, (g) conflict, and (h) convulsion.

a   b

Figure 3.17.   Pathways in space: (a) curving and graceful; (b) punching making straight line.

Have someone demonstrate the various uses of space, time, and energy as you watch. Practice your ability to read feelings as you watch different movements. You can gain additional observational skills by carefully observing people around you. An airport or bus depot is a perfect place to develop expertise in body reading. As you observe, notice how individuals carry the whole body and how movement of separate body parts is integrated into the entire pattern. Those who lean back while they walk, for example, appear slow or carefree; those who tilt forward look like they are in a hurry. People with rounded shoulders and a forward head look depressed. Those with an open chest and outward focus portray a feeling of confidence.

The next exploration has to do with tuning into a subtle use of the elements of movement and feeling these changes in your own body. Begin by forming a circle with other participants. One person initiates the sequence by doing a short action, preferably one that is slow and in which there is no altering of body facing from being inward to the center of the circle. Pass this same movement around the circle. Take care to perform this action in exactly the same way, making no changes in the elements of space, time, or energy. After several movements are passed around the circle, the participants are instructed to make changes in each action as it comes to them. It is a good idea to change only one element at a time, because otherwise the exploration becomes muddled and loses its purpose. Clarity of movement perception, however, is developed by asking individuals to change only the use of space, time, or energy. Let this exercise go on only until people are seeing and altering movement with accuracy.

Learn to tune into your body and its movements. Take your mental focus inward at various times during the day to see which body feelings come forth; these are the things your body is trying to tell you. Doing some inward focusing each day allows you to begin to monitor changes in energy level, centering, and spatial use. Your body is not a constant entity, but a changing integration of systems. Be sensitive to these changes so that you can satisfy your body's needs. Stop an activity or change pace, for example, when your body tires.

Gendlin (1981) has written a book, *Focusing*, in which he describes the process of looking inward, or making contact with a special internal body awareness. Gendlin calls this body awareness *felt-sense* and says that it is an important part of the therapeutic process. The ability to focus and tune into the body can help you change, because it is the body's sense of a situation or problem that initiates awareness of the need to change. It is a message from your body. These messages will not be detailed like verbal communication, but will be of a more global and less distinct form, like a hunch. When such a body feeling comes to you concentrate on it. Usually such body messages are relevant to some event in your life, and the content should become clear as you focus. It is a feeling of the rightness of action in specific situations.

Become aware of subtle variations in nonverbal communication and use this knowledge to your advantage. Carry your body in a manner that displays poise and confidence. Shake hands with a sense of strength. Monitor each of the elements as you sit, stand, and perform other daily activities until you achieve the most effective use of these actions in presenting yourself to the world. Proper use of posture and gesture can allow you to change from a shy, reticent person to one who meets life head on with energy and a positive sense of self.

Dancers use many variations of the elements of movement all the time. Learning to dance means mastering subtle changes in space, time, and energy. Dance skills are developed from a heightened awareness of normal body language. Such abilities take many years to study and perfect. Doing choreography teaches the individual to manipulate the elements for purposes of artistic intent, because a dance communicates nonverbally.

Nonverbal Communication
in Group Movement Experiences

Participation in group movement exploration experiences is one way to gain skill with nonverbal expression. The following exercises also train your perceptual abilities with respect to movement.

Music may be used during some of the explorations. The right kind of music can provide an atmosphere that encourages relaxed concentration and helps to develop rapport among participants. Appropriate music should be quiet, continuous, and played on a few instruments or a synthesizer. Accompaniment with a strong pulse or a defined rhythm often disturbs the ability of participants to focus on self and body. In these explorations music provides background sound. It should set the stage for action, but the movement itself is motivated by body impulses. Meditation music, new age sound, and environmental tapes are usually appropriate in this situation. Many record and tape stores include sections stocked with these kinds of music.

The first exploration involves *following*. It can be done in a large group or with just two people. In either case, one person is leader, and the others follow. The leader has his or her back to the rest of the group. Begin by taking your focus inward; be as relaxed as possible. This action will bring the mind and body together. The leader begins to move slowly after several seconds of focusing. Actions should be simple, and the leader's back remains to the group. If movement goes from side to side, the leader should still have his or her back facing those who are following. Members of the group should concentrate on the leader's whole body and on the various shapes it goes through. Avoid looking at one body part. The more you try this exercise, the easier it becomes; you will find that you do not have to think so much to stay with the movements (Figure 3.18).

Mirroring is another activity involving nonverbal communication. Pair off with someone who is about your height and stand facing that person. Choose one person as leader, and begin again by focusing inward. The other individual must mirror the leader's movements as if he or she were looking in a mirror. If the leader moves on the left side of the body, the follower moves on the right. The leader and the follower must remain facing each other throughout the exercise. Keep the movement simple, and see the action in whole shapes. Do not look at one part of the leader's body at a time. A feeling of concentration and togetherness should develop between you and your partner as you practice this exploration (Figure 3.19).

Figure 3.18. Following leader.

Figure 3.19. Mirroring.

You might like to try some variations on the mirroring theme. One idea is to stand facing your partner and copy the movements in opposition. If the leader moves right the follower moves left; if the leader goes up the other individual goes down; and if the leader advances forward, the follower recedes or reaches backward. This exploration takes greater concentration and is more difficult than simple mirroring (Figure 3.20).

Figure 3.20. Mirroring in opposition.

A second variation is to mirror only after the leader has completed an action. This activity requires that the leader move for a short time and then stop to let the person following complete the pattern. Stopping and starting can interfere with concentration at first, but practice will help you overcome this problem. Delayed mirroring tests your movement memory.

Another possibility is to respond to, rather than mirror, your partner. This exploration is best done standing and facing the other person. Again choose a leader, and when the leader moves, the other person responds with a gesture. Do not think about your responses, just move and respond until a dialogue is going on between the two of you. Change leaders after you have tried this exploration for awhile.

Two people can relate through use of body shape as well. It is a good idea to experiment with individual body shaping before attempting to relate your body placement to that of another person. You can position your body in many ways. Try making it wide, tall and thin, or flat to the ground. Be perceptive concerning the kinesthetic feelings that arise as you go through body shaping. Another method of shaping your body is to put it in symmetrical or asymmetrical positions. (The concepts of symmetrical and asymmetrical body shape were covered under the topic of balance in chapter 2.)

Begin by moving around space, stopping periodically in different body shapes. If you play music, the group can stop at the same time the music stops. After you have experimented with diverse body positions, try moving close to a person near you.

Retain the last shape in which you put your body, and begin to move and shape yourself in relation to the other person. Continue shaping and relating your bodies. A nonverbal dialogue should evolve based on positioning and repositioning two bodies in space. You can extend your creativity by thinking of the number of ways you and the other person can relate through the concept of body shape. For instance, you can move over, under, around, and through the body spaces of your partner. Once you start to move, see how long you can keep this dialogue going (Figure 3.21).

Larger groups of people can also relate through use of body shape. Participants can stop in a shape when the music stops, but then more than two people can bring themselves together. Four to six individuals make a good group size. Begin again with your final body shape and relate through a constantly changing use of body position (Figure 3.22). All people in the group should move at the same time.

The touch dialogue is a takeoff on nonverbal conversation through body shape. In the touch dialogue, two people relate and move by way of touching some part of their bodies. It is best to begin this exploration by touching hand to hand with a partner. For many this is a safe way to get into work involving touch. Put

a   b

Figure 3.21.   Nonverbal dialogue: (a) shaping body to body; (b) another example of shaping dialogue.

Figure 3.22.   Large group relating through body shape.

Figure 3.23.   Moving with fingertips touching.

the palms of your hands together. Focus inward and when you feel the urge to begin, allow movement to happen. The actions should flow like a conversation between two people, rather than having one individual act as leader. You need not remain in one spot or at one level. Take your conversation high, low, forward, backward, diagonally, and on curved pathways. Vary movement speed. It is also interesting to change the pressure of touch be-

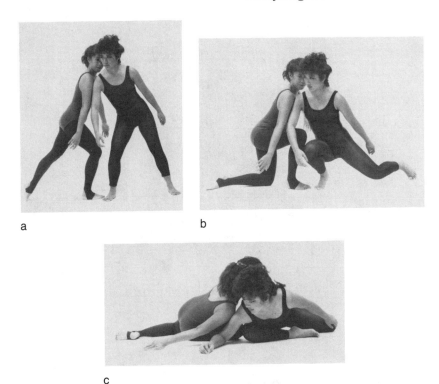

a   b

c

Figure 3.24. Explore movement with other parts of the body touching: (a) begin by contacting shoulders, (b) start to lower weight, and (c) continue to touch but go closer to floor.

tween you and your partner. Changing tactile pressure helps develop kinesthetic sensitivity (Figure 3.23).

The next step is to move and touch different parts of your bodies. The point of contact could be a shoulder, the back, or a foot. You might, for example, put your hand on the back of your partner's lower leg, or your upper arm on his or her back. Be courageous, and try to maintain continuous movement once you have selected a point of contact with your partner (Figure 3.24).

The touch dialogue can be used with groups of more than two people. One way to begin this exploration is to form a circle with participants' fingertips or palms touching. The participants close their eyes and concentrate on their bodies. When the urge to move occurs, go with it, but continue to have contact with the person on either side. The exploration should build in intensity, and then come to a conclusion. Keep the movement fairly slow throughout. It might be a good idea to share individual feelings

Figure 3.25.   Touch movement dialogue in larger group.

a   b

Figure 3.26.   Exploration: (a) counterbalance partner and (b) move to new position still counterbalancing.

about this experience with other group members (Figure 3.25). Try the same exploration with eyes open as a contrast.

Body weight can also provide the impetus for a movement dialogue. Take hold of the hand or wrist of your partner and begin to move so that the two of you are *counterbalancing* each other. Action should be spontaneous, causing you and your partner to reach and stretch in various directions, while continuing to

a   b

Figure 3.27. Contact exploration: (a) assume stance in which one person fully or partially supports another, then (b) move to new position continuing to lend support (movers may change roles, alternately lending and giving support).

counterbalance each other. Change the point of holding contact and continue to move and counterbalance (Figure 3.26).

Contact improvisation provides another avenue for a nonverbal exchange. Here the body of one participant receives the weight of the other. As you move, the point of contact will change as will the job of weight bearing (Figure 3.27). Care should be taken when doing contact improvisation. Try to stay relaxed, and avoid giving the total weight of your body to another.

Chapter Four

Using Kinesthetic Sense and Imagery

There is a definite connection between mind and body. The mind can affect the way the body feels and reacts in various situations. You can analyze movement and learn to act more efficiently. An understanding of the communicative aspects of posture and gesture can also enable you to use the nonverbal to express yourself more effectively. Both of these methods of movement analysis were discussed in chapter 3 and are examples of using the mind to affect the body.

The connection between mind and body can be turned around. What you do with your body and how you treat it can, in turn, influence thought and feeling. Participating in exercise on a regular basis makes one feel good, builds body awareness, and improves confidence. Eating wholesome foods from the four basic food groups each day affects the chemical balance in the body, promoting efficient operation of all body systems and an overall sense of health and well-being.

Holistic health practitioners emphasize the importance of the mind/body connection. Thinking the right kind of thoughts can lead to a life relatively free from illness, stress, and defeat. The attitude is one of seeing life as a whole with the mind and body together. It is the ability to take interest in life, stay focused, and discover a rhythm and purpose for existence (Rose, 1984).

Kinesthetic Sense

What physical sense enables individuals to receive and transmit messages back and forth between body and mind? The body sense is known as the *kinesthetic sense*. It receives messages from the body by way of receptors located in muscles, tendons, and joints. The kinesthetic sense could be compared to the visual sense. The eyes pick up visual messages from the environment, which are then transmitted to the brain. Variations in light rays are relayed to the brain where they are interpreted as visual images. Changes in the body are monitored by appropriate receptors and interpreted as changes in muscle tension and length, body shape and movement, and the relationship of the body to gravity. The kinesthetic sense also operates in activities requiring skills in balance and rhythm. The *proprioceptive sense* is used to include all sensory systems that respond to stimuli arising in muscles, tendons, joints, and the vestibular apparatus or inner ear (Sage, 1977).

Tests of Kinesthetic Skills

There are many tests for visual and auditory acuity, but not very many measures for assessing kinesthetic awareness. Emphasis in our society is on the visual and auditory aspects of the world, whereas the body senses are often overlooked. Kinesthetic ability seems to become important only when it is necessary to learn movement skills like those involved in sports or dance activities.

Watch people in a class where learning a movement skill is the primary activity. You could observe a tennis class or one in aerobics or jazz dance; it doesn't really matter. In each case you will see variations in student ability. Some individuals learn movement patterns with great speed, whereas others need much more time to practice an action after it is introduced. Look carefully at the class, and you will also see a lot of variation in the way sequences are reproduced by each person in the class. Some students change the size, direction, or level of an action. Others alter the timing or application of energy. Review the elements of movement (space, time, and energy) described in chapter 3, and try to see whether individuals reproduce patterns with accuracy in all three areas. If you note changes in movements, decide in which element area changes occur. This is an exercise in training your eyes to see. Movement is transitory. It disappears quickly so observations must be made rapidly. Be patient with yourself as you learn to improve your movement perception.

The *Purdue Perceptual-Motor Survey* (Kephart & Roache, 1966) measures some facets of kinesthetic ability in children. It includes items that assess the kinesthetic accuracy or awareness of the subject. The following paragraph describes some parts of the test that might be interesting for you to do.

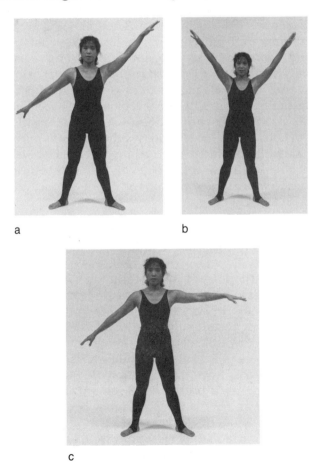

Figure 4.1. Three body positions from Purdue Perceptual-Motor Survey.

In the identification of body part portion of this test, the child is asked to touch specific parts of his or her body, including the shoulders, hips, head, ankles, ears, feet, eyes, elbows, and mouth. Knowledge of body parts has long been recognized as vital to developing space localization. Imitation of movements is done in another portion of this test. Here the individual must imitate the placement and body position of stick figures in order to measure neuromuscular control and translation of visual cues into movement (Figure 4.1). Mirroring exercises and an obstacle course are also included in this survey. The obstacle course aids in determining to what extent clumsiness is a spatial error or a problem in motor control. The *Hill Test of Selected Positional Concepts* (Hill, 1981) is another kinesthetic awareness test. It was designed for blind children as a way of measuring their ability to put specific body parts in a place or position. The following are some examples of items from the Hill test: (a) touch your nose with the middle finger of your hand, (b) touch the finger that is farthest away from your left thumb, (c) put your hand in front of your face, (d) make your heels higher than your toes, (e) put yourself in front of the chair, and (f) put the block over your head. The first two items in this list are thought to measure positional relationships of body parts, the second two the ability to move various body parts in relationship to each other, and the last two analyze ability to move with respect to objects. The Hill test deals with many other items. Sighted people would, of course, do this test with their eyes closed.

Advantages of Kinesthetic Testing

The area of kinesthetic awareness testing has been largely overlooked. Training in some type of sports or dance activity is part of almost everyone's life, yet very few tests exist for basic ability in this area. Such tests could point out talent in kinesthetic awareness—a talent that could be developed through proper training. It could also show where a child was lacking and needed some remedial work. It would be a good idea to use kinesthetic awareness testing as a prerequisite for entrance into college physical education and dance programs. Such testing would allow prospective students to determine the degree of kinesthetic awareness with which they were endowed, and those with low kinesthetic awareness ability could be advised to pursue other kinds of career training.

Perhaps kinesthetic awareness testing will become popular when researchers decide exactly how to define and describe different areas of human knowing. Until recently, studies of learning systems were tied to the visual and auditory senses. Most intelligence testing, in fact, deals only with verbal or mathematical knowledge. Very little testing has been done to analyze more creative or global learning.

Kinesthetic Awareness and Intelligence

In the book *Frames of Mind*, Gardner (1983) explores human potential in terms of multiple forms of intelligence. The book, which is based on Gardner's studies at Harvard and Boston University School of Medicine, includes chapters on linguistic, musical, spatial, bodily kinesthetic, and personal forms of intelligence, among others. The basic premise of this work is that there is evidence for the existence of forms of intelligence that fall outside traditional spheres of testing. Gardner outlines a new theory of human competency that challenges the classical view absorbed from psychological or educational theory. If other forms of intelligence do exist, then the potential of many people is not being thoroughly explored.

People are much alike, and yet they are different. We all exist on the same planet, but the information each of us receives about the surroundings is not exactly the same. This difference is due to the fact that all individuals do not live in the same environment, and so sensory input is actually different, but variation in the ability to analyze sensations from the same environment is also a contributing factor; all people do not have the same perception of input.

Differences in analyzing sensory information are attributed to varieties in perceptual style. For example, in the 1950s Herman Witkin came up with the concepts of *field independence* and *field dependence*. Field-independent people are able to ignore conflicting visual surroundings to find a hidden figure; field-dependent subjects are more influenced by visual surroundings that distract from their finding the same figure (Corsini, 1984). In addition, some psychologists believe that those who participate in like tasks have a similar perceptual orientation; dancers are more kinesthetic and painters more visual (Corsini, 1984).

Imagery as the Link
Between Body and Mind

Human imagination is the link in the mind/body connection. *Imagery*, when used properly, can affect the body, causing changes to occur.

Lulu Sweigard (1974), who was a kinesiologist at Juilliard, developed a system of body learning using imagery. This system, aimed at postural correction, was called *ideokinetic facilitation*. In this system, the learner focuses on a mental image that relates to correct placement or use of the body. No conscious movement is made along with the focusing, because concentration on the right image is thought to trigger appropriate body responses by way of the nervous system. Sweigard believes that an over-emphasis on voluntary efforts is one of the greatest handicaps to efficient motor learning. Telling students how to tighten muscles or hold body parts interferes with the functioning of the nervous system. The nervous system will take care of how a movement is to be done when it is presented with a clear mental picture of that action. Some of Sweigard's images are described in the following sections.

Adelaide Bry (1978) has written a book called *Visualization: Directing the Movies of Your Mind*. Bry discusses many aspects of the mind/body connection and suggests that we use it to improve our health, explore mind potential, and set goals. Bry describes mental visualization as a process in which individuals see pictures in the mind just like movies shown on a screen. Furthermore, Bry believes that such movies of the mind can be used to enhance the way a person lives.

To successfully use the *movies of the mind*, or imagery, one must accept that there is an interaction between mind and body and that the two entities work together (Bry, 1978). Some basis for this belief can be drawn from the work of anatomists who have demonstrated that pathways exist between the part of the brain that stores images and the autonomic nervous system; these same pathways link the autonomic system, pituitary, and adrenal cortex, so that pictures in our mind can affect every cell in the body. Research in biofeedback also shows that we have much more control over parts of the body originally thought to be totally automatic in their operation.

Visual and Kinesthetic Imagery

The mind/body connection makes use of two forms of imagery: visual and kinesthetic. Both types are fun to use and easy to recognize when the difference between them is understood.

Visual imagery is a picture you have in your mind. To be used in motor learning, this picture must relate to the desired shaping or placement of body parts. It must be an image that you can hold in your mind's eye. An example of such an image would be one frequently used in dance classes. A common placement of the arms in dance is to put them in second position to aid balance during the center floor warm-up (Figure 4.2). In second position, the arms are held slightly lower than the shoulders on shallow diagonals in front of the body where they are curved, not straight. One visual image used to describe second position is beach ball arms. In other words, hold your arms as if they encircled a huge beach ball in front of your body. The visual image paints a picture that you can relate to kinesthetically.

Figure 4.2.   Second position, arms and legs.

Kinesthetic images are body feelings that accompany moving or placing the body in a specific manner. The movement must have a certain feeling about it when performed correctly. An example of an action would be to pick the foot up from the floor as quickly as possible and extend the ankle and toes at the same time. A helpful kinesthetic image here would be to pick the foot up as if the floor were hot pavement. This would be similar to walking on a hot sidewalk and trying to avoid excessive contact with the ground. Think back to your childhood and remember how you moved when you were caught in such a situation.

More About Imagery

Mental imagery is a wonderful capacity of the human brain. We experience many mental pictures when we dream, only some of which we remember when awake. As we go through each day, we also experience many diverse images. Life, in fact, seems to exist on two levels: the physical world and the mental interpretation of tangible surroundings. Our interpretations of the world are colored with various feelings, and these are stored in memory. Many memories, in turn, can be retrieved and paraded for review in the motion pictures of the mind. In addition, we understand new information by relating it to earlier experiences. Sometimes this relating is helpful, and sometimes it gets in the way of learning, because it calls forth negative memories—a mental videotape of a bad experience that plays in our head. In either case, each of us has a repository of memories that makes up a unique imagery-filled inner world.

Place your body in a relaxed position and close your eyes. Be sensitive to images as they come to you. You will find that many are from past experiences. You will also discover that one mental picture leads into the next, providing you with a steady stream of changing imagery. Stay quiet for awhile and continue to enjoy the motion pictures playing in your head. As you experience the different pictures, you will notice that they are usually visual. Review the same images and attempt to call forth memories of sounds and body feelings this time, although this may be more difficult than calling forth visual imagery alone. Another way to understand the different forms of imagery is to perform a simple movement and focus on the various kinds of imagery at the same time. In other words, you can see a visual picture of the action in your mind, feel it kinesthetically in your muscles, and imagine appropriate qualities of sound or accompaniment at the same time. To get a full-blown picture of mental imagery, however, it is necessary to draw on all sensory systems of the body.

We can get a lot of information about the *sensory modality* of imagery from research on mental rehearsal of motor skills, although these reports can be confusing. What is interesting is that subjects indicate experiences with all three imagery forms: visual, auditory, and kinesthetic. In many instances, the type of imagery changes with the learning of different movement skills. Imagery preference is primarily visual, auditory imagery was the next most popular form, and kinesthetic images were used the least (Sackett, 1935). On the other hand, none of the three forms of imagery appeared to be superior to the others (Lawther, 1977). Perhaps the best imagery for learning motor skills is a teaching method combining all three forms (Richardson, 1967b). Other writers indicated that the kinesthetic image is the most important to the development of movement ability. The kinesthetic image of a movement must be complete for successful motor performance to occur (Jones, 1965). Cues derived from the other senses must be transferred into cues used to construct the kinesthetic image.

Bandler and Grinder (1979) have made imagery an important part of their approach to communicating with others. They call their method *Neuro Linguistic Programming*, which is based on the premise that people access memories and bring forth images that are connected to different sensory modalities. Some are visual, some auditory, and some kinesthetic. The preferred mode of imaging, according to Bandler and Grinder, makes up that person's representational system. In addition, these two writers believe you can learn about another's imagery preference by watching his or her eye movements. For example, if a person looks up and to the right when asked a question, he or she accesses memories through the visual system. Eye movement to the side indicates a preference for auditory imagery, and movements of the eyes down and to the left mean that the individual is a kinesthetic imager. Watch people as you talk to them and decide which representational system is dominant. Asking certain kinds of questions can help reveal imagery use. Questions about color or shape would illicit answers from visual memory; questions concerning sound or music trigger auditory forms of representation. One of the main points Bandler and Grinder attempt to make is that using the person's preferred representational system can help in communicating with him or her. Teachers, in particular, should realize the importance of communicating through all three sensory channels to best communicate with all members of the class.

All people do not have the same ability to tap into their imagery systems. Researchers have found a variability in imaging capabilities from one person to the next. Some researchers believe that problems in motor skill development can be caused by a lack of efficiency in the learner's imagery systems. Two factors are identified by some as relevant to an individual's ability to use imagery: the vividness and the controllability of imagery (Start & Richardson, 1964). Some people have highly developed, vivid imagery, whereas others create hazy images that are not distinct. The control factor refers to the ability to hold onto or produce images for any length of time. Have a partner suggest different scenes, sounds, and body feelings to you, and see if you can produce the accompanying visual, auditory, or kinesthetic imagery. Compare your images in a sequence to determine clarity or vividness of each.

Some researchers have created tests for vividness and ability to control imagery. Two such tests are the *Gordon Test of Visual Imagery Control* and the *Betts QMI Vividness of Imagery Scale* (see Greenstein, 1979). A problem in ability to control imagery would be a situation in which you could not switch images rapidly, or in which images were hazy. In the Gordon test subjects are asked to visualize a car in 12 different situations and score the imagery quality of each item "yes," "no," or "unsure." The Betts scale has more items than the Gordon test. In this test subjects work with visual, auditory, tactile, and olfactory images that are rated for vividness on a 1- to 7-point scale.

Imagery as an Aid to Body Awareness

Use of visual and kinesthetic imagery aids movement accuracy and body awareness. A return to the same visual picture or body feelings each time you get ready to perform a similar movement should trigger the same muscular response.

Select a movement that you wish to perfect, and have a partner observe your performance. Your partner should be aware of how this movement is supposed to be done. Ask your partner to help you find the correct placement or position; he or she can even guide your body. Do the movement the correct way several times, and connect this performance with appropriate visual and kinesthetic cues. Decide what the movement looks and feels like. Execute the movement again, concentrating on the visual and/or kinesthetic images you have selected. Have your partner observe your performance for accuracy.

Try using these other visual images to motivate movement. Concentrate on the picture of a circle at the side of your shoulder. This circle's radius is the length of your arm. Move your arm through the entire circle several times. Your action should have an even energy flow with the center of the circle located at the center of your shoulder joint. Do not tilt the circle, but keep the plane of action perpendicular to the floor (Figure 4.3).

The center of gravity can be used to motivate visual imagery. Picture your center at the front of your body, and visualize it tracing a straight line in space off to the right or left. This straight line is parallel to the floor. Now actually move your whole body to the side so that the center traces a straight line in space. Next imagine your center as tracing a curved line or a series of scallops as you move to the side. Duplicate these curved shapes by moving your own center to the side. You will find that you have to push off from the ball of your foot preceding each side step and end with feet close together and flat on the floor, knees slightly bent. This scallop pattern is known as an overcurve. The direction of this curve can be reversed and changed to an under-

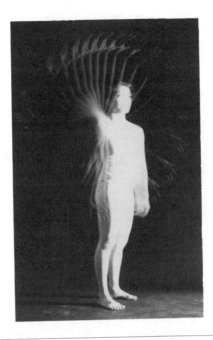

Figure 4.3. Arm circle at right angle to floor.

curve by bending the knees as you step to the side. Each side step ends by straightening the knees (Figure 4.4).

Straight and scalloped lines can also be formed at the side of the body by using the center of the hip as the tracing point. Walk straight ahead maintaining a smooth transition across the floor so that the center of the hip traces a straight line in space. Then see if you can do both overcurves and undercurves drawing with the hips as you move ahead. Decide which form of walking seems more natural to you. Increase the tempo of your walk until it becomes a run. Notice that with each running step the center of your hip makes a scallop in space at your side (Figure 4.5). Attempt to run so that the spatial pathway of the hip is a straight line. You will probably find this more difficult.

Go back to the triangular weight placement of the feet against the floor. This concept was discussed under alignment in chapter 2. Imagine the triangle along the bottom surface of each foot and try to feel it. The inner and outer borders of the ball of the foot are on the floor with the heels touching. Walk across the floor several times emphasizing the triangular placement as the whole foot rolls to the floor. Resist the temptation to roll to the inside or outside of your foot as you walk.

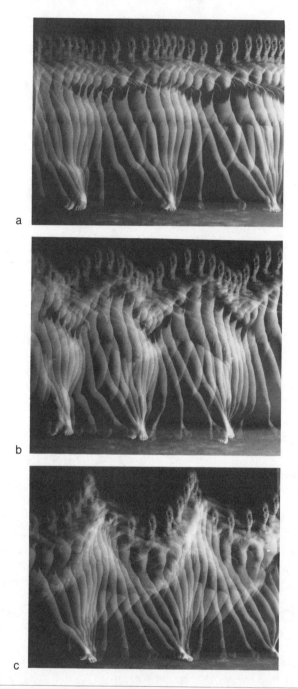

Figure 4.4. Movement of body to side: (a) remaining at same level to floor (head, shoulders, and hips trace straight line in space), (b) changing level (body parts describe overcurve in space), and (c) changing level in different way (body parts describe undercurve).

Figure 4.5. Running step (center of hip traces overcurve).

Look at the space around you and design a floor pattern for your steps. This pattern could be made up of curved or straight lines, or it could combine the two types of lines. Figure 4.6 illustrates some potential floor patterns. Once you have chosen a floor pattern, see it in your mind's eye. Walk through the floor pattern initially, and then retrace this same design using other kinds of locomotor steps such as run, hop, jump, slide, leap, and gallop. Practice the same floor pattern again, changing to different locomotors at various places in the same design so that you do more than one locomotor step throughout.

It can be fun to experiment with kinesthetic imagery. Stand with your feet slightly apart and with the toes of both feet pointing straight ahead. Imagine that you have a large mass of taffy in your hands and that you are pulling this taffy, making it stretch and then allowing it to contract. Visualize that your legs are taffy; flex and extend the leg joints as if they are made of this pliable

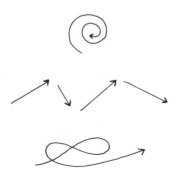

Figure 4.6. Three different floor patterns.

substance. Do this leg action several times, feeling the plasticity of motion.

Maintain the same leg and foot position you used in the previous exploration. Imagine what your body would feel like if it were suspended in air, arms and legs dangling downward. Try holding yourself up with your body suspended beneath you. Identify the kinesthetic feelings you discover in this situation, and see if you can duplicate them while standing on the ground. Hold on to the feeling of being suspended as you practice this method of standing.

Hands are remarkable and capable parts of the body. Move one hand for several minutes to explore the movement possibilities; then try the following actions. Put the palm of your hand on a table and move only the fingers one at a time (Figure 4.7). This motion is similar to drumming the fingers on a table, except that the fingers remain nearly straight rather than bent at the knuckles. Next, place all fingertips on a surface with joints extended, and draw the fingers back, flexing them toward the center of the palm. Repeat the action of reaching the fingers out and drawing them inward (Figures 4.8 and 4.9). Finally, move the palm along the surface of the table by flattening it and then sliding the heel of the hand up to meet the fingers. You can move the palm all the way across a surface using this reaching/sliding motion . As you rehearse each of these hand movements, focus on the kinesthetic feeling that predominates in each. See if you

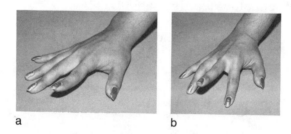

a   b

Figure 4.7. Exploration of movement potential in hand: (a) lift index finger, then (b) lift second finger.

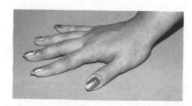

Figure 4.8. Another exploration of hand: begin with hand flat.

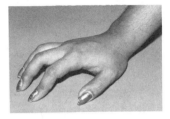

Figure 4.9. Slowly draw fingers toward heel of hand.

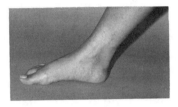

Figure 4.10. Exploration of foot: begin with foot flat.

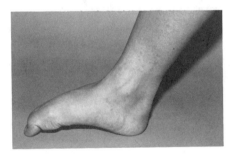

Figure 4.11. Draw toes toward heel.

are able to transfer these actions in Figures 4.8 and 4.9 to your foot (Figures 4.10 and 4.11).

Walking on various kinds of surfaces has a different kinesthetic feeling about it. Try walking on a rug, the sidewalk, and grass. How accurately can you describe how each type of walking feels in your body—particularly in your feet and legs? Visualize another kind of surface and imagine the feeling of walking on it. The image of walking on a pile of fallen leaves is fun to work with: picture the leaves in your mind, and then walk as if the leaves were really underfoot. Practice imaginary walking in mud, on ice, and in water as a contrast. Each image should provide a different muscular response so that the changes in kinesthetic sensation affect the kind of walking that occurs.

The movement quality of your arms also depends on the environment. You would, for example, move your arms one way in water and another in air. Imagine that you are standing in a swimming pool with water up to your neck. Think about the feel and consistency of the water and the way in which it resists the actions of your arms. Actually move your arms at the side of your body while concentrating on the image of passing through water. Do real movement of your arms in the air as a contrast. Note the sense of lightness when you move through air. Concentrate on the image of standing in a substance heavier than water, perhaps gelatin, and discover how to move your arms in this situation. Transfer the various kinesthetic feelings you experienced to movements in other parts of your body.

Lifting or pushing objects of a different weight and density can alter movement quality. Pretend to push a very heavy object. Try pushing a heavy object as practice if you are not sure of how your body feels in this situation. Be aware of the increased effort and muscular tension involved. Then return to pushing while using the image alone as motivation. Visualize other objects of diverse structure and weight, and do real movement as you pretend to push them. Some suggestions for objects to push are a feather, a clothes tree, a chair, and a large wad of plastic. Differentiate among the kinesthetic feelings that accompany pushing in each situation.

Using Imagery to Improve Alignment and Movement

Imagery—both visual and kinesthetic—is used in various ways to correct alignment and improve movement efficiency. Each of these techniques is discussed in the following section.

Anatomical Imagery

Anatomical imagery is based on a sound understanding of body structure. The size and shape of the bones that make up the skeleton as well as the joints where bones articulate were discussed in chapter 1. The muscular system was also a part of the same discussion. The point is to retain a clear mental picture of body structure to work with anatomical imagery. It requires concentrating on body structure and how it moves or is positioned. These images of movement or placement are believed to trigger correct use of the body. The following anatomical images were designed to enhance posture and are based on the lines of movement found to exist in a well-aligned body. The lines of movement were intended to function between specific skeletal parts with each line beginning and ending in a bone. Those practicing these visual cues must visualize the image only; no attempt is made to manipulate body parts to achieve good alignment (Sweigard, 1974). The words in parentheses describe the body position in which Sweigard believed each line of movement would be most successful in realigning the body. The visualizations have been created by the author.

1. Shorten the distance between the midfront of the pelvis and the 12th thoracic vertebra. Visualize a shortening between the midfront of the pelvis and the 12th thoracic vertebra (standing).

2. Widen the distance across the back of the pelvis. Watch the width at the back of the pelvis grow broader (any position and walking).

3. Lengthen the central axis of the trunk upward. Visualize a lengthening of the central axis of the trunk upward (standing or sitting).

4. Extend the pelvic spine downward. See the pelvic spine lengthening downward (constructive rest position; Figure 2.42).

5. Elongate the line from the center of the knee to the center of the hip joint. Imagine a line from the center of the knee to the center of the hip as growing longer and moving more deeply into the hip joint (constructive rest position).

6. Lengthen the distance between the top of the sternum and the top of the spine. Visualize a lengthening in the line between the top of the sternum and the top of the spine (constructive rest position, sitting, and standing).

7. Narrow the front of the rib cage. See a narrowing of the rib cage at the front of the body (constructive rest position, sitting, and standing).

8. Narrow the width in front of the pelvis. Watch a narrowing at the front of the pelvis (constructive rest position, sitting, and standing).

9. From profile view, bring the ankle closer to the line of gravity (Minton, 1981). Imagine the ankle moving closer

into alignment with the body's line of gravity (standing). (Note: I adjusted this last line of movement for purposes of my doctoral dissertation project.)

Other experts in the dance field have worked with anatomical imagery. Solomon (1987), for example, believes that the key to teaching dance successfully is using visual imagery as the descriptive language. This use of imagery indicates what is happening in the body as it moves and is based on anatomy as used by the medical profession. Anatomical terms and images are used to depict the mechanics of movement with students. An example of Soloman's approach to teaching dance movement follows.

> Standing relaxed, with feet in parallel position, arms above the head . . . we curve the lumbar spine back, keeping the shoulders over the hip sockets and bending the knees as needed to deepen the curve. . . . This articulation in the lumbar area allows the spine, lumbar through sacrum and coccyx to form one continuous curve, the lower end of which, if extended forward in im-

a   b   c

Figure 4.12. Exploration of body: (a) begin with body straight, arms overhead; (b) curve lumbar spine backward, keeping shoulders over hips; (c) return to original position.

agination between the legs, would strike the floor. . . . By keeping the shoulders over the hip sockets we cause the dorsal spine to reflect the curve below it; hence, the entire spine, up through the cervical curve is drawn into one continuous arc [Figure 4.12]. (Solomon, 1987, p. 51)

Pictorial Imagery

Sweigard (1974) devised many pictorial images she believed encouraged good alignment. Many of the pictures are comical, but are at the same time based on the lines of movement she believed are present in good posture. In these exercises, students do no movement, but concentrate only on the suggested images.

One of these mental pictures involves imagining the pelvis as a ball of ice cream on top of a cone with the legs taking the place of the cone. At first the cone is tipped down in front so that the ball of ice cream bulges forward. The idea here is to watch the front of the cone move up to a level position allowing the ball of ice cream to fall back into place inside the rim. This visualization

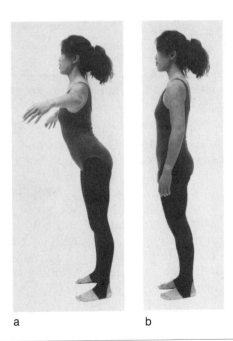

a   b

Figure 4.13. Visualizations to improve posture: (a) incorrect position in which lumbar spine is hyperextended; (b) the image of shortening between midfront of pelvis and 12th thoracic vertebra can help correct problem (concentrate on image, do not attempt to move body parts).

is done in standing position and works to shorten the distance between the midfront of the pelvis and the 12th thoracic vertebra (Figure 4.13).

Another of the pictorial images can be practiced while sitting, standing, or walking. In it, you see two hip pockets at the back of your pelvis that are slowly moving around to the front of your body (Sweigard, 1974). This visualization is supposed to produce a broadening at the back of the pelvis. To lengthen the central axis of the body upward, Sweigard suggests that you imagine your neck growing like Alice in Wonderland's neck. This exploration can be done standing or sitting and should raise the head to a higher level. To lengthen the pelvic spine downward, visualize each side of the pelvis as if it were a revolving paddle wheel. The wheel turns backwards, upper sides moving toward your heels (Figure 4.14). The constructive rest position is recommended here.

Figure 4.14. Pictorial image of paddle wheel revolving backwards (used to reduce pelvic tilt and lengthen spine downward).

To narrow the front of the rib cage, see it as a small accordion with handles on each side of the body under the arms. The vertical pleats are located on the front and back of the ribs. The idea is to watch the accordion close inward toward center until it is no wider than the neck (Sweigard, 1974). This exercise can be used in constructive rest and while sitting and standing. Narrowing the width at the front of the pelvis can be accomplished by pretending there are two elephant ears, one on each side of the pelvis. Watch in your mind's eye as the two ears fold tightly across the front of the hips. Constructive rest position is recommended for this visualization.

Kinesthetic Imagery

Many helpful images are kinesthetic and involve seeing or feeling patterns of energy throughout the body. In her book *Teaching Young Dancers*, Lawson (1975) makes many suggestions to reeducate muscles through dance training. Most of her ideas have to do with stretching or lengthening muscles. She talks about lifting the rib cage, stretching upward through the rectus abdominis, and drawing the buttocks muscles toward the coccyx.

Another energy image is more internal. To correct alignment, Dowd (1981) imagines that there is a lake in the pelvic floor, and beneath the lake is a fissure through which a volcano erupts. The fire of the volcano creates steam that sends a geyser out of the mirrored surface of the lake, out through the center of the torso, up through the top of the head, leaving a veil of spray all around the body. The energy pattern is up through the center of the body and down the outsides.

Body Image

The concept of body image has been discussed by psychologists and dancers for many years. It refers to the ability to picture your own body in your mind's eye. Some people have a negative body image, whereas others carry around a mental picture that is incomplete, blocking out parts of their body from the whole picture. We receive sensations such as tactile, thermal, and pain from our bodies. Messages also come from the muscles and viscera. Beyond these sensations, however, an experience that the body is a unity provides knowledge of position and posture; it is a schema called *body image* (Schilder, 1950).

Think about the image that you have of your body. There may be parts you block out and that are not an integrated part of the whole image. Perhaps you have negative feelings about these parts of your body, or perhaps you do not think about them much. It is common to mentally block out body parts one cannot see. The whole back side of the body, for example, is not readily visible unless you look at it in a mirror.

Some graduate students in dance have done interesting research dealing with body image. Many of these studies used emotionally disturbed individuals as subjects and others used college students. The goal of these studies was to see if participation in dance improved body image. The nature of an individual's body image was evaluated with tests such as the *Karen Machover Draw-A-Person Test* and the *Secord-Jourard Body Cathexis*. The Draw-A-Person test is used as an indicator of completeness of body image. In this test, the subject is given a paper and pencil and asked to draw a person. This test is then scored in terms of completeness, facing, sex, and size of drawing. The Body Cathexis evaluates the feelings of satisfaction and dissatisfaction with particular body parts. The data collected in one study done in the dance department at University of California at Los Angeles indicated changes in body image following participation in a dance class (Sare, 1969).

You can do some work with your own body image. Lie down on the floor or sit quietly in a chair. Close your eyes and focus on your body. Mentally scan your entire body. Find places you think about a lot and parts that rarely enter your conscious thoughts. Focus on one part of your body usually not in awareness, like your back, and visualize it, examining it in great detail. Psychologist Jean Houston (1982) suggests that you use body image to improve your own body. She recommends that you scan the entire body beginning with the feet. Great care should be taken to see the body parts in the mind's eye; notice spaces between your toes, the shape of your ankles, and the connections between body parts. Mentally scan until you have covered the entire body, and then imagine how you would like your body to be. See it first and then jump into this ideal image. Many people have found fixing their attention on the ideal body is an excellent way to control weight.

Mental Rehearsal

Mental rehearsal is an imagery technique that makes use of body image to improve motor skills. In this method the individual reviews the performance of an action, sports skill, or dance sequence in the mind. The goal is to see yourself performing the desired movements effortlessly and in the correct manner. Many believe that mental rehearsal releases impulses over motor pathways, making use of natural forms of movement and incorporating these actions in the execution of a desired motor skill (Lawther, 1977). Mental rehearsal produces a new coordination because it is thought to trigger the appropriate muscles that alter a movement problem (Richardson, 1967b). Others believe that mental practice operates by activating the brain rather than the neural pathways (Jones, 1965). In either case, researchers have found that this technique produces an action potential in the muscles that would normally have performed the visualized movement (Sage, 1977).

Some authorities have challenged the use of mental practice during early learning, saying that students benefit from this training method only when mentally reviewing physically familiar tasks (Richardson, 1967b). Other researchers found people could use mental rehearsal to improve movement skills they had never done, because these skills were somehow integrated into the imagination to produce a passable performance (Start & Richardson, 1964). The best motor learning, however, seems to result from participating in a combination of both mental and physical practice (Richardson, 1967a).

Pick a movement or sports action that you want to perfect. Read about the correct performance of this action, or, better yet, watch a skillful execution of this movement sequence. Next, visualize yourself as you do an effortless execution of the same skill.

Houston (1982) has stated that mental rehearsal improves self-concept and body awareness; she uses a system called the *kinesthetic body*. To work with the kinesthetic body, you select an action and perform it. Doing is followed by imagining the movement being done by the kinesthetic body or body image. Each of Houston's explorations is preceded by relaxing, closing the eyes, and focusing inward. Two of Houston's exercises follow.

> Raise your real right arm and stretch. . . . Feel the stretch in your fingers, your hand, your arm, your shoulder, your torso. Now, with equal awareness, lower your arm.
>
> Repeat this several times.
>
> Now stretch your kinesthetic right arm, allowing yourself to experience this as vividly as possible. (p. 16)

Houston follows the same procedure with a fencing lunge.

> Now with your real body, make a fencing lunge to the right [Figure 4.15].
> Come back to center.
> Repeat this several times.
> Now lunge to the right with your kinesthetic body. (p. 16)

Creative Movement Experiences

A mental picture or kinesthetic idea can motivate you to move in many ways, because the nature and feeling contents of images differ. Again review a series of images in your mind, and try to verify the feeling state that accompanies each. Remember that alterations in feeling state can change the posture and movement of the body. A shift in imagery can cause changes in the elements of movement incorporated in an action because different images are colored by diverse feelings. Resulting movements relate to a feeling, whether it is real or imagined.

a   b

Figure 4.15. Fencing lunge: (a) beginning position and (b) lunge.

Practice concentrating on an image that has a strong feeling for you. Start to move once you are involved in the image, but be aware of the kind of movements that come forth. Work with this image until you have exhausted the possibilities for movement. Think back to the information offered in chapter 3 on the connection between feeling and body language if you have problems making the connection between your imagination and movement triggered by your imagination. Remember that shifts in mood cause changes in posture and gesture. If you feel differently, you will alter your use of the elements of movement. Each image you select should have a feeling state about it; you need to focus on this feeling when you are involved in exploring the image. Select another image—one that contrasts with the feeling tone of the first image. Allow yourself time to focus, and begin to move again. The quality of movement should be different in this second experience. Compare the two explorations to determine if there are differences in use of the movement elements of space, time, and energy when you are involved in moving in relation to the second image.

Creative movement experiences involve a stimulus and a movement response. The leader presents suggestions that he or she thinks will initiate movement in members of the group. The suggestions given by the leader are motivations for movement. Each stimulus, as it motivates movement, is connected with some type of imagery and subsequent feeling. The imaging is the link between stimulus presentation and the resulting creative movement quality.

Think of a suggestion that could trigger movement. It might be a color, a sound, or an object. Concentrate on the stimulus and then allow yourself to move freely. Do not attempt to think through patterns before acting. Try several short movement experiences, being sensitive to the process of creating. You will discover that before you can move you first must have some kind of feeling/image of the movement—an image that is a generalization of the original motivation. This generalization is based on the feeling state connected with the motivation. A diagram of the creative movement process would include motivation, to feeling/image, to action (Hawkins, 1964). It is also necessary to tap memories from past experiences as part of this creative process, because you understand each new stimulus in terms of feelings and situations from your own life.

In creative movement experiences, each stimulus has the capacity to trigger certain forms of imagery. The stimulus and consequent imagery can be classified according to one of the human sensory systems. The following groupings of motivations for creative movement are arranged with reference to each of the sensory systems.

Visual stimuli include shapes, colors, lines, and designs (Figure 4.16). Pictures, objects, and forms from nature are also examples of visual motivations for movement. Different pieces of construction paper cut into a multitude of shapes provide a wide variety of colors. Linear designs can be collected from books and magazines, or you can draw them yourself. Pictures can also be collected. Many small objects such as sculptures, leaves, feathers, flowers, shells, or pine cones are excellent movement stimuli. The idea is that each stimuli evokes a different feeling state, resulting in different imagery. Changes in feeling state cause a change in movement quality (Hawkins, 1964). Although individual differences exist, red usually instigates fast movement; blue is slow. A spiral line design indicates a curved use of space, and a straight line is to the point.

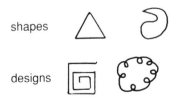

Figure 4.16.   Design as stimuli for movement (different designs change perceived feeling and thus movement response).

Finding auditory stimuli is also simple. Check your record and tape collection for recordings that have sounds of varied quality. These could be metrically organized music, electronic sounds, or environmental recordings. Words have different qualities that can be exaggerated, and poetry, when read aloud, contains many different feelings as well.

Kinesthetic stimuli may be more difficult to discover due to our tendency to ignore the body and movement. Various body feelings such as tall, thin, wide, and flat are grouped here. The loco-motor movements walk, run, hop, jump, slide, leap, gallop, and turn provide a direct kinesthetic response, as do action words like dart, collapse, melt, jiggle, soar, push, and float.

One human modality we often overlook is the tactile sense. We touch things all the time, but ignore the resulting sensations and feelings, unless they point to emergency situations (e. g., a hot handle on a pan). Tactile sensations can be a rich source of move-ment stimuli. Begin to notice all the textures that surround you. Each has its own special quality that can be translated into cre-ative movement. Rough textures generate movement in vibra-tions or short spurts of action. Smooth surfaces call for gliding motion, and soft objects such as a puff of cotton generate light, floating movement.

The next step in the progression of relating stimuli and move-ment response is to work from purely image-motivated begin-nings. Here, creative movement is triggered by imagery alone. No object or picture is used as a step preceding the resulting imagery.

Some general suggestions for the use of creative movement stimuli follow. It is helpful to begin such sessions with time for focusing. Relaxation exercises can be used to focus, or the time can be spent simply looking inward. The goal in either case is to encourage an atmosphere of tuning into the body and strength-ening the mind/body connection without distraction.

Stimuli for movement have the best effect when arranged in sequence so that participants move from one stimulus to the next, until the whole series is completed. Adequate time must be provided for exploration between the presentation of each stimulus. The first stimulus should be more superficial or out-ward directed, with later motivations being more feeling-oriented and meaningful (Hawkins, 1964). It is uncomfortable for many people to be involved at a feeling level in the beginning of any activity, and work with creative movement is no exception. People need time to get their feet wet before plunging in. Reveal-ing feelings in any form is a very personal and sensitive area. An example of a more outward-directed motivation is a linear design, whereas reacting to a picture is more inward in its orientation. A picture as a stimulus for creative movement would cause you to connect with more personal memories and associated feelings as a basis for movement. A single movement session could include stimuli from different sensory areas, or from a single modality. The choice is up to you or your group leader. In either case, attempt to combine stimuli in different ways, choosing from a variety of sensory areas.

Other Avenues of Exploration

As a dance person, I have long believed that a connection exists between the diverse avenues of sensation/perception. The creative movement experiences described in the preceding section are part of the training of most modern dancers. Moving in a way that an object feels to the touch or appears to sight is a common experience in dance education. It is training directed at similarities rather than differences between sensory areas. These similarities are not highly detailed and specific, but more general or global in nature.

Evidence for the existence of an underlying similarity between sensory modalities exists in both the arts and psychology. In the next two sections, these concepts are discussed in terms of both the senses and the right brain.

Connecting the Senses

Many artists speak about a connection between the senses by comparing qualities in their work to traits common to other art forms in a different medium. Painters Paul Klee and Wassily Kandinsky both thought their paintings were endowed with musical qualities. Kandinsky spoke of an inner vibration as part of the creative process. Painting, he said, occurred as a harmonic process (Lassaigne, 1964). Klee created many of his pictorial images through the use of line. Some believed that he used line in an active way, molding it as a musician manipulates sound like a polyphony around a firm melody (Haftmann, 1954).

Psychologists also talk about connections between the senses. They call these connections *synesthesia*, which is the experience that the visual appearance of one thing reminds you of the sound, taste, or smell of something else. Synesthesia is a crossing over between the senses, creating a connection with the essence of each thing perceived. In synesthesia, sounds are seen and smells are heard, whereas feelings can be perceived visually (Rivlin & Gravelle, 1984). The most common crossover between the senses is between hearing and vision; people who have this capacity even agree that specific colors and images are evoked by certain sounds.

There are many ways to help you understand this connection between the senses. One of these is a tactile exploration activity. It can be done while staying within the confines of one room, or traveling from one space to another. The goal here is to explore your environment through touch. Two people need to work together in this exploration. One person closes his or her eyes, while the other person leads that person around the space to be explored (P. Berg, personal communication, summer, 1986 [class notes]).

The leader encourages the other person to touch surfaces and objects that have a variety of textures. Care is taken to keep the person doing the exploration from bumping into obstacles or from moving too quickly. As you touch different objects, you need to get involved in the unique tactile quality of each. Visualizing the object at the same time connects the experience with the sense of sight. You will find that some visual-tactile connections are easy to judge; others are much more remote. Both people should have a chance to do this exploration.

Association by color provides another method of making sensory connections. For this exploration, think of an event from your past. It could be something you did or somewhere you traveled. Decide how you feel about this event and choose a color that best fits the image in your thoughts (D. Johnson, personal communication, winter, 1987 [class notes]). Go through a series of images and come up with a color association for each. These images could also be people or objects from your past. Write down the color you associate with each image, or have a number of color samples from a paint store so that you can select the colors from a varied assortment (Johnson). Make your color choices quickly without thinking about them for a long time. Review your choices and the images that stimulated each decision, and see if there is any pattern in the associations. If possible, compare your choices to the choices of others around you.

Drawing or scribbling to music provides for associations between the senses by making a response to sound visible. Find some paper and play several pieces of music with different feeling qualities. As the music is played, draw your immediate response to the sounds (Hawkins, 1964). Felt-tip pens of varying colors work well in this exercise. It is important to draw without altering or judging your drawings as you do them. Compare the drawings after you have done them. You should notice a contrast in line quality from one drawing to another. Think about each piece of music, and then look at how it motivated you to draw. Some of your scribbles may have more flexible or curved lines; others will be more direct or zigzag in design. If other people are doing this exploration with you, compare your drawings to theirs and note similarities and differences.

Tapping the Right Brain

Many authorities in the arts and psychology believe that the human brain has two modes of operation: the *right* and the *left brain*. In most people the left brain is involved with language, logic, reasoning, numbers, and analysis; the right brain with rhythm, music, imagination, images, colors, and pattern recognition (Buzan, 1983). The left brain is linear, working with one piece of information at a time, whereas the right brain is global in approach. To explore the full potential of the mind means to use both sides of the brain. In his book *Use Both Sides of Your Brain*, Buzan (1983) makes this point by describing how great scientists and artists were "both-brained." Individuals such as Einstein and da Vinci indicated in their notebooks that they were motivated by images and global concepts, but the realization of a theory or the execution of a work of art took a carefully thought-out process that preceded step by step in a linear fashion.

In her book *Drawing on the Right Side of the Brain*, Edwards (1979) discusses the use of the right brain to improve drawing ability. The right brain, she says, is better with spatial problems. It perceives relationships between shapes and how parts go together to make up the whole. The right brain is the seat of dreaming, visualizing, and imagining.

There must be a shift to the right brain mode if it is to be used successfully. This is a shift into a more subjective state of mind where feelings of being connected, timeless, and confident exist. You are absorbed and at one with your work and the environment. It is a very pleasurable state of mind in which to find yourself.

Edwards (1979) believes that the way to trigger the left-to-right-brain shift is to present the brain with tasks that appeal to the right brain alone. In these tasks, students are encouraged to draw using global, not finite, methods. Emphasis is put on recognizing shapes, relationships between shapes, and negative spaces between shapes, and then transferring these perceptions to the drawing pad (Figure 4.17).

Figure 4.17.   Negative or empty spaces exist between body parts.

You can use the right brain to become more aware of your body and improve movement ability. The creative movement explorations described earlier in this chapter dealt with the left-to-right-brain shift, because creative movement incorporates imagery, a right brain concept.

Develop your abilities of perception and learn to see through the right brain mode. When you are learning a movement skill, begin to observe the whole sequencing and connecting of separate actions. Notice where in space the movement pattern begins and how it comes to a conclusion. Throughout the pattern the body goes through many shapes, body parts trace pathways in space, and negative spaces appear and disappear along the way. The next exercises are designed to emphasize body learning by way of the right brain mode.

Stand facing a partner. The leader puts his or her body in a shape. Any shape will do. After the leader finds a shape, try to duplicate it with your own body. Continue shaping and copying until it becomes automatic. Resist the temptation to see body parts one at a time, but see relationships between parts instead. Figure 4.18 shows the individual moving through some body shapes that emphasize the relationship of parts. Doing this exploration more rapidly may help you concentrate on total body shapes rather than separate parts of the body.

Figure 4.18. Moving body passes through many shapes.

Edges of the body trace pathways in space as you move. Work with a partner. Watch your partner move one body part through space. See if you can mirror this pathway using the edges of the same part of your body (Figure 4.19). Practice working with pathways until you feel comfortable with this exploration. Have someone move in a dark room while he or she holds a flashlight in

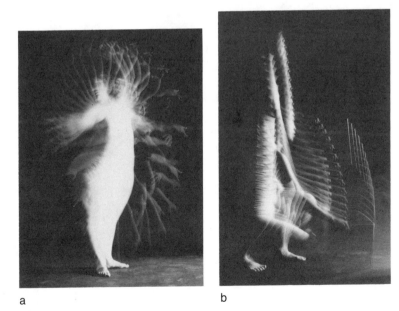

a   b

Figure 4.19. Arms and body describe decorative pathways in space: (a) curved and (b) more straight.

one hand. The designs traced in space as the flashlight is moved from one point to another should be evident (Figure 4.20).

Figure 4.20.   Flashlight demonstrates spatial pathway or action.

Epilogue

The progression followed in this book extends from the physical and tangible to the less concrete. Basic anatomy is discussed first, followed by an analysis of basic movement principles. More intangible material is covered in chapter 3 as movement efficiency is described together with the feeling aspects of gesture and posture. Each of these areas—movement efficiency and expression—is described in the context of the elements of movement. Chapter 4 explores uses of the imagination to connect mind and body and enhance self-awareness.

Much of the information included in this work is part of basic dance training. The hope is that the reader will be able to incorporate it into daily life as an enlightened way of seeing, feeling, and moving in the world. Successful use of these materials requires learning how to focus and look inward. In writing this book, I had to decide on the meaning of the information in terms of my own life, and thus the process of writing became a learning experience. Each reader will have to do the same, exploring the connections between self, personal experiences, and the content and ideas found here.

It is my hope that this book will provide possibilities for self-exploration. Life can truly be an adventure if one learns to listen to the inner self and connect it with the infinite variety found in the world outside. There is a certain strength to be discovered in this connectedness.

Glossary

---

abduction—Movement away from the midline of the body.

adduction—Movement toward the midline of the body.

aerobic—Form of exercise that develops cardiovascular endurance.

Alexander Technique—Body therapy system that deals with realigning the body, particularly through repositioning the head.

alignment—Placement of the body's segments one above the other as closely as possible to a straight line that extends at a right angle to the floor.

aliveness—Quality that contributes to the dynamics and projection of a movement.

angular movement—Movement in which body parts trace a curved pathway in space in an arc or circle.

arcing—Basic movement used in Aston Patterning. It involves rounding and straightening the lumbar and sacral spine while the individual is seated on a chair.

art—Creative work that incorporates principles such as form, unity, and beauty. The arts usually include painting, sculpture, architecture, music, literature, drama, and dance.

Aston Patterning—Body therapy system that works to release habitual tension patterns in the body.

asymmetrical—Unbalanced body shape of one or more people.

awareness—Alertness to or consciousness of something.

axis—Point or center around which an angular movement takes place.

balance—State of equilibrium.

ballistic movement—Bouncing movement.

base—Part of the body on which the whole body rests.

biofeedback—Technique for helping people reduce arousal or stress.

body image—Image or picture one has in the mind of one's body.

body level—Receiving information from the body.

body type—Shape, configuration, or makeup of the body.

cartilage—Tough, white, elastic animal tissue.

cartilaginous joint—Joint or articulation that permits only slight movement, but that is very strong. It is formed from the union of bones with intervening discs of fibrocartilage.

centering—Process of locating both the physical and the psychological centers of the body to achieve a feeling of being aligned and together.

center of gravity—The most dense part of the body located slightly below the navel. The center of gravity is usually lower in women than in men.

center of weight—Same as the center of gravity.

cervical spine—The part of the spine that makes up the neck. The cervical spine curves forward and is made up of seven separate vertebrae.

coccyx—The bottom-most part of the spine, sometimes called the *tailbone*.

communication—Giving out or receiving information.

compensation—Balancing technique in which one body part is counterbalanced by movement or shifting of another body part in an opposing direction.

concentration—Focusing or fixing attention.

concentric—Form of muscular contraction in which fibers actually shorten in length.

connective tissue—Tissue that acts as a binder and support of various structures in the body.

constructive rest—Position of the body thought to encourage relaxation.

contact improvisation—Spontaneous movement drawn from actions done while relating to the environment, or while in contact with another moving body.

contraction—Shortening fibers within a muscle.

control—The ability to direct the actions of the body and execute them in a desired manner.

core—The most central part of an idea or work of art.

counterbalance—Offsetting the weight of one part of the body by the opposing weight of another body part in order to achieve balance.

curvature of the spine—Distortion of the natural alignment of the spine usually in a sideways or lateral direction.

curves of spine—Natural forward and backward bending of the spine that helps to counterbalance the weight of the various body segments.

dance—Movements of the body in rhythm, especially to music.

dance education—Process of developing movement skills and creative movement ability through certain techniques or strategies.

direction—One aspect of the movement element of space. There are eight basic directions in which the individual can move or face the body.

dorsiflexion—Movement of the ankle in which the angle at the front of the joint is decreased.

eccentric—Type of muscle contraction in which there is a lengthening of fibers.

ectomorph—One of the three basic body types that is long, lean, and loosely strung together.

elements—The three basic components of movement—space, time, and energy or force (shape is at times a fourth element).

endomorph—One of the three basic body types that is soft and rounded and has an excess of fatty tissue.

endurance—The ability to last, continue, or go on moving.

energy—One of the elements of movement; movement is motivated by energy.

essence—The intrinsic or fundamental nature of something, as a work of art.

eversion—Movement of the bones in the foot and ankle so that the sole of the foot lifts up and faces outward.

fatty tissue—Connective tissue formed from fat cells in a meshwork of other kinds of tissue.

feeling—An emotion.

felt-sense—The body or general feeling that arises concerning a question or situation.

felt-thought—The body or general feeling that arises and precedes your ability to verbalize a thought or idea.

fibrocartilage—Anatomical structure made up of cartilage and also a large amount of fibrous tissue.

fibrous joint—Very strong and immovable joint. The connecting bones are held in almost direct contact by a thin layer of connective tissue.

field theory—Theory of the psychology of perception based on ability to separate self from nonself, or to distinguish between different but related ideas.

flexibility—Range of movement allowed in the various joint areas in the body. Muscular tightness and structural traits both limit flexibility.

flexion—Movement in which the joint angle narrows.

flow—One of the categories of effort/shape analysis having to do with the use of energy in the body.

focus—To concentrate on sensations and feelings arising from inside oneself.

force—One of the elements of movement; force propels action (used in exchange with the word *energy*).

frontal plane—One of the three planes of movement that extends to the side from the midline of the body.

Gestalt therapy—Therapy based on principles of being in the present and becoming aware of it. The client is encouraged to discover blocks to awareness by fully experiencing current thoughts, feelings, and body sensations.

gesture—Movement of the body or of a part of the body that expresses feelings or ideas.

gravity—Force that draws all bodies in the earth's sphere toward the center of the earth.

grounded—To be centered, stable, and integrated in mind and body.

group movement—To move in relation to another person or persons. This requires taking cues from the actions of others.

habitual patterns—Customary ways of performing everyday movement such as walking and sitting.

Hill Test—Test of kinesthetic ability designed for blind children.

holding pattern—An organization of tensions that is held in muscles.

holistic health—Approach to a state of health that connects mind and body and requires a positive attitude.

horizontal plane—One of the three planes of movement that is parallel to the floor.

hyperextension—Movement in which the joint angle widens and the action goes beyond normal extension.

ideokinetic facilitation—Process of concentrating on the image of a movement or position with the idea of allowing the central nervous system to choose the most efficient neuromuscular coordination for performance. No voluntary movement is involved.

image—Visual representation or picture that can be held in the mind.

imagination—The act of forming mental pictures of that which is not actually present.

intelligence—The ability to understand experiences; performance of certain tasks (in this context, it refers to mental as well as other capacities).

inversion—Movement of the bones in the foot and ankle so that the sole of the foot lifts up and faces inward.

involvement—The state of having one's attention occupied; movement experiences requiring more than a superficial level of attention.

joint—A place where two bones articulate. Joints vary in their potential for movement.

kinesiologist—An individual who studies and is knowledgeable in the science of movement mechanics.

kinesiology—Movement science that studies the mechanics of movement in relation to human anatomy and physics.

kinesthetic—Relating to the aspects of kinesthesia or the sensation of position, movement, or tension. In this text it also means motivation for movement.

kinesthetic ability—Degree to which an individual senses body position, movement, or tension.

kinesthetic body—Secondary, nonphysical, subtle body similar to the body image; the picture of your body encoded in the motor portion of the brain.

kinesthetic sense—Human sense which monitors body position, movement, or tension.

left brain—It has been discovered that the human being has two upper brains that operate differently. In most individuals, the left side of the brain is responsible for linear and analytical thought.

level—One aspect of the movement element space. There are three basic levels: high, middle, and low.

lever—A rigid bar that has an axis of rotation; a point at which force is applied; a resistance that must be overcome. The human body has many levers.

ligament—Band of tough tissue that connects bones or holds organs in place.

linear movement—A movement in which body parts (or the whole body) trace a straight line in space.

line of movement—Imagined lines of energy extending between specific points in the body and relating to good alignment.

locomotor—Movements that cross space.

lumbar—Part of the spine that makes up the small of the back. The lumbar spine curves forward and is made up of five separate vertebrae.

mass—Quantity of matter forming a body of a certain shape and size.

meditation—Reflecting or looking inward.

mental rehearsal—Reviewing movements and procedures in the mind without participating in overt actions.

mesomorph—One of the three basic body types that is husky, large boned, and has thick muscles.

midline—Imaginary line that cuts down the center of the body, separating right side from left.

mind/body—Concept that the mind and body are not separate, but intimately related.

mind's eye—Place in the mind where visualization seems to occur.

mirror—Copying the movements of another while facing that person.

modality—Different sensory systems such as vision, hearing, and so forth.

momentum—Impetus of a moving object.

motor learning—Relatively permanent change in motor behavior resulting from practice or experience, and not based on maturation.

movement exploration—Process of coming up with or creating movement based on ideas, stimuli, or images presented by the teacher or leader.

movement potential—Movement range or possibilities to be found in the various joints of the body.

movement principles—Fundamental laws of movement education such as the basics of aligning the body or of moving in relation to gravity.

movies of the mind—Picturing or visualizing ever-changing images in the mind that allows you to tune into your inner awareness and feelings.

muscle—Body organ consisting of bundles of fibers that can contract and expand to produce movement.

music—Arrangement of vocal and/or instrumental sounds to form a structurally complete and expressive composition. Different pieces of music vary in terms of factors such as melody, harmony, rhythm, and timbre.

nervous system—Body system consisting of the brain, spinal cord, and peripheral nerves that transmits signals to muscles to produce movement.

Neuro Linguistic Programming—Explicit model of human experience and communication that can be used to describe human activity, allowing for deep and lasting changes.

nonverbal—Without spoken or written words.

nonverbal communication—Form of communication that does not use words.

organic—Creative product that has an interrelationship or organization of parts similar to that of living things.

pantomime—Use of actions or gestures without words as a method of expression.

passive—Person (or object) who is influenced or acted upon, but who does not exert influence or react.

pathway—Designs traced on the floor as an individual travels across space; designs traced in the air through movement of various body parts.

pattern—Arrangement or organization of parts or elements.

perception—Awareness of objects or other kinds of data through use of the human senses.

perceptual style—Particular emphasis put on sensory data. Some individuals, for example, rely more on visual data, whereas others tune in more readily to sound.

physique—Structure, form, or appearance of one's body.

plane—Taking place in only two directions or dimensions; to be flat and not three-dimensional.

plane of movement—Particular plane in which a movement occurs.

plantar flexion—Movement of the ankle so that the toes reach out and the ankle straightens or extends.

plumb line—Device consisting of a string with a weight on the end of it; often used to judge posture from a profile view.

progressive relaxation—System created by Edmund Jacobson and designed to rid the body of tension by developing a sensitivity to tensions where they exist.

projection—Throwing energy outward from one's body, giving a quality of aliveness to movement.

pronation—Movement in which the foot rolls inward on the arch, or in which the hand is placed in a palm-down position.

proprioception—Complex set of sensory receptors located in muscles, tendons, joints, and the inner ear that monitors body movement in relation to muscle tension and position.

Purdue Perceptual-Motor Survey—Survey instrument developed to qualitatively assess the perceptual motor abilities of children in early grades.

quality—Movement characteristics as determined by use of body energy.

realign—Bringing the body into improved alignment or posture.

reciprocal innervation—Stretching technique based on contracting one muscle or muscle group against resistance, releasing that group, and then stretching the opposite muscle or group.

relaxation—Making less firm or tense.

repatterning—Altering habitual ways of moving or holding the body.

rhythm—A structure of patterned movement through time.

right brain—Capacity of the human brain to think in a global manner, emphasizing spatial relationships and imagination.

rotation—Movement that twists around the long axis of a bone or of the spine.

sacral—Part of the spine that makes up the back of the pelvis and has fused rather than movable vertebrae.

sagittal plane—One of the three planes of movement that extends to the front and back from the midline of the body.

schema—The image one has in the mind of his or her body.

segment—Any of the parts, such as the head or forearm, into which the body is divided.

sensation—The process of receiving impressions and input through the body's various sensory organs.

senses—The body's facilities for receiving impressions and information.

sequence—Series of movements in an ordered progression.

shape—Interrelated arrangement of body parts of one person or group of persons.

size—One aspect of the movement element space; size can vary from a very small to the largest possible movement.

skeleton—Bony framework underlying more superficial parts of the body.

skill—Ability or proficiency, particularly with movement.

space—One of the elements of movement, which occurs in and across space.

spinal cord—The part of the nervous system that runs through the center of the vertebrae of the spinal column.

strength—State or quality of greater power developed by causing muscles to do more work.

stress—Accumulation of tension in the body.

stretch—State of greater range of motion developed through lengthening of muscles.

supination—Movement in which the foot rolls to its outer border, or in which the hand is placed in a palm-up position.

symmetrical—Balanced body shape or grouping of individuals.

synesthesia—Experience of a stimulus producing secondary and subjective sensations in a modality not being stimulated.

synovial—Type of joint that allows for freedom of movement and has a space between articulating surfaces of bones.

tendon—Inelastic cords made of tough fibrous connective tissue, in which muscles end and by which they are connected to bone.

tension—State of mental or nervous strain, usually accompanied by muscular tightness.

thoracic—Part of the spine that makes up the chest area. The thoracic spine curves backward and is comprised of 12 separate vertebrae.

time—One of the elements of movement.

tissue—Any of the structural materials making up an organism and having a particular function.

unity—State in which there is a sense of whole or fitting together.

verbal—Use of words, particularly for purposes of communication.

vertebrae—Separate bones that make up the spinal column.

visual—Connected with or used in seeing.

visualize—To hold a picture in the mind.

weight—Quality of heaviness; the part of the body where the heaviness is supported takes the weight.

Bibliography

Alter, J. (1983). *Surviving exercise*. Boston: Houghton Mifflin.

Arnheim, R. (1964). *Art and visual perception*. Berkeley: University of California.

Bandler, R., & Grinder, J. (1979). *Frogs into princes*. Moab, UT: Real People.

Barham, J. (1978). *Mechanical kinesiology*. St. Louis: Mosby.

Brown, B. (1980, Fall). Is contact a small dance? *Contact Quarterly*, p. 7.

Bry, A. (1978). *Visualization: Directing the movies of your mind*. New York: Barnes and Noble.

Buzan, T. (1983). *Use both sides of your brain*. New York: Dutton.

Clippinger-Robertson, K. (1986). Kinesiology and injury prevention. *Journal of Physical Education, Recreation and Dance*, **57**(5), 50-53.

Corsini, R.J. (Ed.) (1984). *Encyclopedia of psychology*. New York: Wiley.

Delsarte, F. (1887). *Delsarte system of oratory*. New York: Werner.

Dempster, W.T. (1955). *Space requirements of the seated operator* (WADCTR 55-159). Wright-Patterson Air Force Base, Ohio.

Dowd, I. (1981). *Taking root to fly*. New York: Contact Collaborations.

Edwards, B. (1979). *Drawing on the right side of the brain*. Los Angeles: Tarcher.

Ellfeldt, L. (1967). *A primer for choreographers*. Palo Alto, CA: National Press.

Fitt, S. (1987). Corrective exercises for two muscular imbalances. *Journal of Physical Education, Recreation and Dance*, **58**(5), 45-48.

Gardner, H. (1983). *Frames of mind*. New York: Basic Books.

Geelhaar, C. (1973). *Paul Klee and the Bauhaus*. Greenwich, CT: New York Graphic Society.

Gelb, M. (1981). *Body learning*. New York: Delilah.

Gendlin, E. (1981). *Focusing*. New York: Bantam.

Greenstein, M. (1979). *Towards optimal functioning: A study of imagery and movement behavior*. Unpublished master's thesis, University of California at Los Angeles.

Haftmann, W. (1954). *The mind and work of Paul Klee*. New York: Praeger.

Hawkins, A. (1964). *Creating through dance*. Englewood Cliffs, NJ: Prentice-Hall.

Hendricks, G., and Wills, R. (1975). *The centering book*. Englewood Cliffs, NJ: Prentice-Hall.

Hill, E.W. (1981). *The Hill Performance Test of Selected Positional Concepts*. Chicago: Stoelting.

Hinson, M. (1977). *Kinesiology*. Dubuque, IA: Brown.

Houston, J. (1982). *The possible human*. Los Angeles: Tarcher.

Humphrey, D. (1959). *The art of making dances*. New York: Gove.

Jacobson, E. (1929). *Progressive relaxation*. Chicago: University of Chicago Press.

Janson, H. (1963). *History of art: A survey of the major visual arts from the dawn of history to the present day*. Englewood Cliffs, NJ: Prentice-Hall.

Jones, J.G. (1965). Motor learning without demonstration of physical practice, under two conditions of mental practice. *Research Quarterly*, **36**, 270-281.

Kapit, W., & Elson, L.M. (1977). *The anatomy coloring book*. New York: Barnes & Noble.

Kephart, N., & Roache, E. (1966). *The Purdue Perceptual-Motor Survey*. Columbus, OH: Merrill.

Lassaigne, J. (1964). *Kandinsky, biographical and critical study*. Cleveland: World Publishing.

Lawson, J. (1975). *Teaching young dancers*. New York: Theatre Arts.

Lawther, J.D. (1977). *The learning and performance of physical skills* (2nd ed.). Englewood Cliffs, NJ: Prentice-Hall.

Lee, M., & Wagner, M. (1949). *Fundamentals of body mechanics and conditioning*. Philadelphia: Saunders.

Luttgens, K., & Wells, K.F. (1982). *Kinesiology* (7th ed.). Philadelphia: Saunders.

Minton, S. (1986). *Choreography: A basic approach using improvisations*. Champaign, IL: Human Kinetics.

Minton, S. (1981). *The effects of several types of teaching cues on postural alignment of beginning modern dancers: A cinematographic analysis*. Unpublished doctoral dissertation, Texas Woman's University, Denton.

Minton, S. (1984). *Modern dance: Body and mind*. Denver: Morton.

Penrod, J., & Plastino, J.G. (1980). *The dancer prepares* (2nd ed.). Palo Alto, CA: Mayfield.

Perls, F., Hefferline, R., & Goodman, P. (1951). *Gestalt therapy: Excitement and growth in the human personality.* New York: Dell.

Richardson, A. (1967a). Mental practice: A review and discussion: 1. *Research Quarterly,* **38**, 95-106.

Richardson, A. (1967b). Mental practice: A review and discussion: 2. *Research Quarterly,* **38**, 263-273.

Rivlin, R., & Gravelle, K. (1984). *Deciphering the senses: The expanding world of human perception.* New York: Simon and Schuster.

Rose, N. (1984). Teacher as healer. *Healing Currents,* **8**(1), 8-9.

Rugg, H. (1963). *Imagination.* New York: Harper & Row.

Sackett, R.S. (1935). The relationship between amount of symbolic rehearsal and retention of a maze habit. *Journal of General Psychology,* **13**, 113-128.

Sage, G. (1977). *Introduction to motor behavior: A neurological approach* (2nd ed.). Reading, MA: Addison-Wesley.

Samuels, M.D., & Bennett, H. (1973). *The well body book.* New York: Random House/Bookworks.

Sare, D.S. (1969). *Changes in body-image and self-concept: A modern dance experience.* Unpublished master's thesis, University of California at Los Angeles.

Schilder, P. (1950). *The image and appearance of the human body.* New York: International Universities.

Solomon, R. (1987). Training dancers: Anatomy as a master image. *Journal of Physical Education, Recreation and Dance,* **58**(5), 51-56.

Start, R.B., & Richardson, A. (1964). Imagery and mental practice. *British Journal of Educational Psychology,* **34**, 280-284.

Sweigard, L. (1974). *Human movement potential: Its ideokinetic facilitation.* New York: Dodd, Mead, & Co.

Todd, M.E. (1975). *The thinking body* (4th ed.). New York: Dance Horizons.

Zorn, J. (1968). *The essential Delsarte.* Metuchen, NJ: Scarecrow.

Index

(Pages in italics indicate figures.)